"THERE ARE TWO COMMUNITIES IN
NORTHERN IRELAND, different in their
origins, nursing different historical
myths, possessing distinguishable
cultures, having different songs and
heroes, and wearing different denomina-
tions of the same religion. Religion is the
clearest badge of these differences.
But the conflict is not *about* religion. It is
about the self-assertion of two distinct
communities, one of which is dominant
in the public affairs of the province."
— *The London Times,* August 30, 1969.

To Betty and Kathleen
with appreciation for their love and support

Conflict and Christianity in Northern Ireland

by Brian Mawhinney and Ronald Wells

William B. Eerdmans Publishing Company

Photos for the cover and body supplied by
"Popperfoto," London.

Library of Congress Cataloging in Publication Data

Wells, Ronald A   1941-
    Conflict and Christianity in Northern Ireland.

    1.   Northern Ireland.   2.   Christianity—Northern
Ireland. I. Mawhinney, Brian, 1940-   joint author.
II. Title.
DA990.U46W44   941.6   75-8948
ISBN 0-8028-1608-8

CONTENTS

Preface　7
1　A History of "Troubles"　13
2　The Burden of Northern Ireland
　and Its Meaning for America　43
3　Life in Northern Ireland　73
4　The Relevance of Christianity　112
Suggestions for Further Reading　126

ACKNOWLEDGMENTS

This book is not an exception to the rule that when any book is published many people deserve recognition for their assistance in helping the authors' ideas assume their present form. Because the authors live and have worked on two different continents, there are some people whom we would like to thank jointly, while others individually.

We express thanks to: our wives, Betty Mawhinney and Kathleen Wells, for their patient encouragement throughout the writing of, and especially for the typing of, the manuscript; to the helpful staff at William B. Eerdmans Publishing Company, especially Marlin Van Elderen, Reinder Van Til, and Joel Beversluis.

Brian Mawhinney expresses gratitude to all those Christians in Northern Ireland, and in particular his parents, who taught and demonstrated to him the relevance which faith in Jesus Christ has to every aspect of life. Ronald Wells acknowledges with gratitude: Calvin College, and in particular William Spoelhof and John Vanden Berg, President and Dean, respectively, for a leave of absence which allowed him to continue his work; The Institute of United States Studies at the University of London, and in particular Esmond Wright and Howell Daniels, Director and Secretary, respectively, for providing a place at the University where this and other work began; his colleagues at Calvin College, especially George Marsden, Henry Ippel, George Monsma, Richard Mouw, Nicholas Wolterstorff, George Harper, and Stanley Wiersma, both for their encouragement and for their assistance in aiding the development of his thinking on an integrated approach to the problem of Christianity and culture.

PREFACE

THIS BOOK will consider the problems of Northern Ireland from a Christian viewpoint rather than a political one. In attempting to focus the issues for a reading public in the United States, Canada, Britain, and Ireland, the authors will suggest that, whether or not people are Christians, they are rightly concerned about the present "troubles" in Ulster and about the future of the province's relationships with Britain and with the Republic of Ireland. It is our conviction that such concern can be most constructively channeled if it can be understood that a root cause of the problems of Northern Ireland is that there has been too much "religion" and too little Christianity. While we will need to discuss politics, economics, and diplomacy, we will nevertheless bring those points to bear upon a basic question: How can the people of Northern Ireland extricate themselves from an historic situation of bitterness and hatred in which religious affiliations have become the emblems of the conflict? Naturally, if peace is to be achieved in Ulster it will require political and social change, and we do not close our eyes to the necessities of such change. But we would add a suggestion for peace that follows Dietrich Bonhoeffer's notion of "religionless Christianity" — a kind of Christianity that transcends the sectarian divisions imposed by decisions made in the impenetrable past. The essence of the gospel, after all, is that God's work in the world gave the potential for all men to be reconciled to each other and to their Creator.

While the authors are two Christians who happen to be Protestants, we hope and believe that we have given neither a "Protestant" nor a "Catholic" viewpoint here. We do not view Irish history in sectarian terms, and we hope to provide a critique of the important issues which all Christians can share. The contributions of the authors reflect their respective backgrounds and concerns. Ronald Wells is an American, a native of Massachusetts now living in Michigan. He sees the problems of Ulster in the context of the North Atlantic culture, which was internationalized by the folk migrations of the nineteenth century. His contribution offers thoughts to Americans and Canadians on how to view the Northern Ireland conflict from a North American perspective. In doing so he gives a mixed review of the ideas of Senator Edward M. Kennedy, despite the fact that the Senator is a leader who enjoys Wells's confidence and for whom he has voted several times. Brian Mawhinney is a Briton, a native of Northern Ireland now living in London. He presents a brief history of Ireland that will suggest the long-standing nature of the "troubles," and an analysis of the difficulties in overcoming that historic consciousness. He also discusses how Protestants and Catholics view each other and their ways of life in order to show how the current protagonists arrived at their entrenched positions. The final section, on the relevance of Christianity to Ulster's future, is an effort by both authors.

We have no easy solutions to offer. Like others who have studied Northern Ireland's history, we are struck by the sheer length of time during which the peoples there have been divided. It would surely be naive of us to think that we, at long last, could offer the talisman that would bring peace to a troubled land. This book will succeed in its purpose, however, if readers are helped to deepen their awareness of the particulars of the "troubles"— particulars that are essentially variations on the theme of the human condition for which Christianity has a remedy. It is difficult to tell now what social and political arrangements will obtain in Northern Ireland when its people have reached the end of the road of justice, toleration, and peace. Our hope is that this book might somehow aid the initial steps down that road.

Conflict and Christianity in Northern Ireland

1 A HISTORY OF "TROUBLES"

SOME PEOPLE INSIST that the beginnings of the "Irish problem" are traceable to 1916. Others would claim that 1690 is a more appropriate date. In fact, the arrival in Ireland of England's Henry II in 1172 first wove together two of the four strands that constitute the background of today's troubles. Henry brought his considerable army to Ireland as a precautionary measure because some of his barons had already settled in parts of that country and had become local rulers. Henry, fearful lest any of them should become too powerful and so threaten the throne, used his mighty visual aid to remind English and Irish alike that he was still the supreme power in the land. Since that day England has been involved in Ireland—as a civilizing or an oppressing force, depending on one's point of view.

Henry's excursion also introduced the religious connection. The Celtic Church at that time, while formally recognizing the authority of Rome, was both weak and independent. Reform, if it was to take place, needed the backing of a strong secular government. The Pope therefore gave Henry's visit his official blessing in the hope that the king would set up a permanent, albeit foreign, administration. Thus, religion and its relationship to the state became a sensitive issue early in Irish history.

Having exerted rather than established his authority in Ireland, Henry turned his attention to other matters. Consequently, his influence and that of his successors began to wane until, by the middle of the fourteenth century, only about one-third of the country, mainly centered around Dublin, was ruled by the English crown. That is to say, most of Ulster, Munster, and Connaught had reverted to Irish control. The English finally determined to stop the erosion of their power, but their policy lacked both the imagination and the drive necessary to tame the Irish. Put simply, the English problem was this: wherever Irish and English intermingled, the Gaelic influence eventually predominated and the English were absorbed. Their "solution" to the problem was the age-old one of separation, which was formally proclaimed in 1366. In that year a parliament was held in Kilkenny under the direction of the Duke of Clarence, son of King Edward III. The statutes it enacted touched most aspects of the peoples' lives. They make interesting reading, for in them one can visualize the difficulties the two communities had in living together. They included measures to improve the defenses of English-held territory, to prohibit private warfare, and to regulate trade. At the level of interpersonal relations, however, the restrictions imposed are even more revealing. Intermarriage between the communities and the fostering of each other's children were forbidden. (The number of interfaith marriages in Ireland today among the descendants of these two cultures is still very small.) The statutes also forbade the English, and those Irishmen who wanted to live with and as the English, to use the Irish language, names, laws, or dress. They even banned the Irish practice of bareback horse riding. Finally, they re-enacted existing laws that excluded the Irish from cathedral chapters and religious houses.

The picture that emerges is one of a beleaguered and insecure English community among an alien people—

people not so much intent on driving them out as swallowing them up, identity and all. In the light of this, it is worth noting how routinely these statutes were ignored. In fact, the church apparently exerted a greater influence on the people to obey the laws than did the state. The bishops threatened to excommunicate any who broke the laws, whereas the state had to import civil servants from England to administer them, so widely were they flouted even by those whose job it was to enforce them. England's concern over her role in Ireland was obviously justified, but the separatist statutes of Kilkenny proved inadequate to safeguard English interests. One hundred years later, on Henry VII's accession, the area of English dominance in Ireland, "The Pale," had shrunk considerably.

THE TUDOR PERIOD

The accession of the Tudors to the English throne made little immediate difference in Ireland. Effective power remained in the hands of the earls of Kildare during the latter part of the fifteenth and early sixteenth centuries. This power was not democratic in nature but stemmed from ownership of large tracts of land and from political astuteness. The latter had caused them to enter into alliances with many neighboring Irish chieftains in an attempt to establish a durable peace. As a result, they were a natural choice to be the king's deputies in Ireland and to govern the country for him.

Periodically, and for various reasons, the earls forfeited the royal favor and were removed from their governing position. During one of these interludes an important political event took place. In 1494, Sir Edward Poynings, the temporary deputy, called a parliament in Drogheda. From it issued a law that was to govern Irish politics for the succeeding three hundred years. Poynings' Law, as it was called, prohibited the meeting of any Irish parliament without the prior consent of the king and council in England. Such consent, they made clear, would not be given unless they were first told why parliament was being called and what bills were to be presented. This law made the Irish legislature essentially subservient to the English, and it was bitterly resented by many people. Thus, in a new and lasting way politics, along with foreign intervention and religion, became the third strand that bound the two communities together in discord.

The English reconquest of Ireland started to gather momentum during the reign of Henry VIII. His coronation as King of Ireland in 1541 put Anglo-Irish relations on a totally new footing. It formally committed the king to Ireland in a way that had not bound his predecessors. At the very least, he was now obliged to defend and protect his fellow countrymen in that land. How much wealth he could recoup from Ireland also became a matter of royal concern. In Ireland the coronation radically affected the heads of family clans, whose ancestors had always been supreme in their own land. It forced them to seek an accommodation between Henry's authority and their natural desire to remain in local control.

Henry chose the policy of "surrender and regrant" as the instrument by which he tried to implement his authority. Under it, the Irish chieftains surrendered their land to Henry, thereby acknowledging his leadership. He immediately regranted it to them to administer on his behalf, thereby protecting the chiefs' positions in their own communities. In an effort to guard against any undue independence by the Irish, a few restrictions were written into the regrants. The chieftains were not allowed to maintain private armies without the king's permission. In this way their potential ability to make trouble for Henry was greatly reduced. Secondly, they were forced to follow and obey English customs and laws. By these means Henry attempted to persuade them to "think English" and to accept England's claim to rule them.

Yet in the long run Henry's policy was as ineffective in subduing and integrating Ireland as were the statutes of Kilkenny, and for much the same reason. They were both English policies that took no account of Irish tradition. Henry's problem was that the idea of primogeniture—the understanding that when a leader dies he is succeeded by his son—which was at the heart of his policy, was foreign to the Irish. He had hoped, by including it, to ensure that the act of surrender would be honored through each succeeding generation. Irish chieftains, however, were traditionally men who had enforced their supremacy over all other claimants. Their rights to the land they ruled "went with the job" and were certainly not hereditary. When they tried to make them hereditary, it was not long before the rank and file Irish rose up in opposition. They saw in the alliance between king and chieftains a move to deprive them of their land. And in their view, any policy that cost them land, their only source of wealth, was a bad one—one to be resisted.

On the religious front, Henry's policy of "Catholicism without a pope" caused little stir in Ireland. The Irish chiefs felt no particular obligation to a pope, and the Anglo-Irish were prepared to follow the lead of their English brethren. Thus, both were content to support Henry's desire to be royally supreme over the church. In fact, the effect of Henry's edicts on the grass-roots level of Irish religious life was minimal. The Irish Church was weak because of internal dissension and poor because its ecclesiastical dues were often difficult to collect in a war-torn land. Many of its churches were in ruins or in poor repair, and the religious teaching and ministering to the peoples' needs were undertaken mainly by itinerant friars. These clerics remained unaffected by Henry, since he produced no one to take their place. Even "his" English Bible and later Edward's English prayer book were in a language the Celtic people did not understand. So religious life continued largely unaffected by the major theological issues of the day.

When Elizabeth I came to the throne, she caused the Irish to accept her Protestantism by having it adopted by a parliament that met in Dublin in January 1560. The political consequences of this establishment of a Reformed church were soon apparent. First, the papacy, which had been England's ally in Ireland for the four hundred years since Henry II, became her enemy. Secondly, the new church attracted few supporters, and as a result Elizabeth's authority was decreased. To most of the natives and the Anglo-Irish its organization and form of worship were foreign, and they preferred to continue to practice their own religion under the guidance of Jesuit priests who had come over from the continent. These priests developed strong personal ties with their parishioners and exercised great influence at the local level. (This ability to identify with and influence people locally still characterizes Irish Catholic priests today.) The net result of the Reformation in Ireland, therefore, was more political than religious and very enduring. For the first time it caused the native and Anglo-Irish populations to work together to such an extent that, outside the Pale, national sentiment became associated with Catholicism. Today, four hundred years later, the association is still strong.

Elizabeth launched the third attempt by English monarchs to come to grips with governing Ireland. After the failures of the two Henrys, Elizabeth tried the policy of plantation. This involved taking land out of Irish ownership and giving it to English and Scottish settlers—those loyal to the crown—who were "planted" in it. The policy was first enforced in 1567 when, after the queen's armies had quelled a rebellion by local chiefs in Munster, large tracts of their land were confiscated and assigned to Englishmen. Elizabeth expected to apply her policy even more rigorously in Ulster after The O'Neill, Ulster's premier chieftain, rebelled because of his increasing distaste for English laws, the Reformed Church, and the erosion of Gaelic traditions. Following O'Neill's victory over Sir Henry Bagenal at the battle of the Yellow Ford, Elizabeth sent the Earl of Essex to Ireland with twenty thousand men to reassert her authority. This he did in a long war of attrition, which ended six days after Elizabeth's death in 1603. Thus, the accession of James I to the English throne marked not only the end of the Tudors but also the end of the reconquest of Ireland.

1603-1800

Although Hugh O'Neill was defeated in 1603, the plantation of Ulster did not start until 1607. It was made possible by what has since become known as "the flight of the earls." The earls of Tyrone and Tyrconnell, two of Ulster's most important earls, decided that their postwar position had become impossible. While they had been allowed to retain their vast estates, they nevertheless felt that their power and independence were gone. In September 1607, they embarked for Europe, perhaps to seek military aid, taking many of their allies with them. Immediately their flight was interpreted as evidence of treason, and their estates—covering the counties of Armagh, Fermanagh, Londonderry, Tyrone, Cavan, and Donegal—were seized by the crown. Into these counties were shipped both English and lowland Scots settlers. The latter brought with them their own brand of Protestantism—Presbyterianism. The counties of Antrim and Down, on Ulster's east coast, were not included in the plantation; they had already been settled by people from the "mainland." Finally, in 1609-10, the city of Derry was "planted" by City of London companies, who changed its name to Londonderry. As a result, city companies enjoyed extensive privileges in that area, including effective influence within the Church of Ireland.

It is not hard to understand why the native Irish resented having their lands, and thus their wealth, confiscated and given to English intruders with a foreign culture and religion. Perhaps it was at this point historically that the whole question of wealth, and subsequently economics, became the fourth strand in the web of issues that together form the basis of the present difficulties.

Sir Thomas Wentworth, who was the king's deputy in Ireland from 1632-40, increased the alienation between the counties still further. He harried the Ulster Protestants because of their sympathy for British Puritans, and he provoked the Catholic natives by continually seeking ways to deprive them of their land. However, his main contribution to the growing discord between the Irish and English was in the field of trade. He actively discouraged the Irish wool industry, one of her few thriving industries, for no apparent reason other than to protect its English counterpart. This in turn increased Irish economic dependence on England, a dependence that still lies at the heart of the Irish problem.

During the decade 1640-50, two significant events took place in Ireland, the first of which left a continuing legacy of bitterness. This was the advent of Cromwell. He landed with twelve thousand men in Dublin in August 1649, as Lord Lieutenant of Ireland, to reconquer the country after the uprising of 1641. Although he remained for only nine months, the cruelty and brutality of his methods, especially his sacking of Drogheda and Wexford after the garrisons in those towns had refused to accept his terms, have not been forgotten. These events still form part of the anti-British bias within Irish Catholic folk history. The reason is threefold. First, it was primarily they who suffered under Cromwell; Protestants had rallied to his cause. He was further disliked by Irish Catholics because the "liberties" for which he fought excluded the liberty of saying mass—on penalty of death! Finally, he saw himself as the instrument of God's wrath and judgment against them, even while he was putting two thousand of "those barbarous wretches" to the sword in Drogheda.

The second significant event of the 1640s was the establishment of a permanent Scottish Presbyterian ecclesiastical system in Ireland. For the first time the Protestant faith was formally divided. Thus, by 1660, Ireland had three main religious groups: Anglicans, Catholics, and Protestant Dissenters, each characteristic of an historically different group of people and each viewing the other two groups with suspicion and distrust.

The economic realities of life were made abundantly clear to the Irish during the latter part of the seventeenth century. The English parliament passed self-protective laws that excluded Irish cattle from the English market, restricted Irish trade with the American colonies, and further restricted their wool industry. Because the deprivation of market outlets was so serious, some people claimed that these acts, plus the flow of money to absentee English landlords from their poor Irish tenants, was a deliberate attempt to keep Ireland poor and subservient. Whatever the English motivation, Irish resentment continued to grow.

James II fled to France in December 1688. Four months later, William and Mary were pronounced king and queen. These two events formed the prelude to one of the most famous milestones in Irish history. On his accession, James had made the brother of the Catholic Archbishop of Dublin Earl of Tyrconnell, and had sent him to Ireland as his representative. By this act early in his reign, James had made clear his attitude toward the Irish. He needed their support for political reasons and devised his policy accordingly, despite the desire of a majority of Englishmen to maintain a Protestant ascendancy in Ireland. Within a short time Protestants were removed from the army, and Catholics were appointed judges and given control of restyled municipal corporations. Thousands of Protestants, apprehensive of the new policy, flocked to England to help in moves to dethrone James. Thus, it was not surprising that James, when he had collected an army with which to attempt to regain the throne he had lost during the English revolution, should start his campaign in Ireland. It was equally natural that the country's Protestants should unite to oppose him. Since most of the Protestants were in the north, the main opposition was centered in Ulster—most famously behind the walls of Londonderry and Enniskillen.

English troops arrived in August 1689 to raise the siege of Londonderry, and they, along with the Protestants, held off James's troops until William landed the following June. On July 1, 1690, William and James, the latter's army supplemented by an additional seven thousand troops from France, met and fought on the banks of the River Boyne near Drogheda (now celebrated on July 12th each year, due to a calendar change). James's army was beaten, and subsequently it was decisively defeated at Limerick in October 1691. Because of the strength of religious feeling at the time, and because the politics of both William and James were intimately bound up with religious principles, William's victory was quickly credited with having rendered Catholics inferior in Ireland. The Protestant ascendancy was vindicated and assured for many years, and mythology and history combined to form the basis of today's religious intolerance.

This Protestant domination, bolstered by much overtly discriminatory legislation, was not undermined until the nineteenth century. Acts were passed that effectively excluded Catholics from the Irish Parliament and curtailed their right to acquire or lease land. Their inferior position was further underscored by the requirement that they pay tithes to the Church of Ireland. Nor were they the only unhappy citizens, for sacramental tests imposed

Nowhere is the link between political and religious Protestant-ism more clearly identified than on the banners of the Orange lodges. One such banner is here reproduced on a wall in a loyalist area of Londonderry.

during Anne's reign debarred Dissenters along with Catholics from public service. Thus the ascendancy, Anglican in character and socially divisive by nature, flourished in discontent and in increasing poverty that was made worse by further trade restrictions around the turn of the century. The very success of these discriminatory laws caused another significant change in Ireland. The numbers and influence of the Catholic gentry were so reduced that their role as political leaders and spokesmen was assumed by the clergy. Ironically, the laws thus tended to establish the powerful influence of the church they were designed to stop.

Jonathan Swift, writing in 1727, gave a graphic description of conditions in Ireland:

> It is manifest that whatever stranger took such a journey (through Ireland) would be apt to think himself travelling in Lapland or Iceland, rather than in a country so favoured by nature as ours, both in fruitfulness of soil and temperature of climate. The miserable dress, and diet, and dwelling of the people; the general desolation in most parts of the kingdom; the old seats of nobility and gentry all in ruins and no new ones in their stead; the families of farmers who pay great rents living in filth and nastiness upon buttermilk and potatoes, without a shoe or stocking to their feet, or a house so convenient as an English hogsty to receive them— these may, indeed, be comfortable sights to an English spectator who comes for a short time to learn the language, and returns back to his own country, whither he finds all our wealth transmitted.

England, by right of conquest, exercised authority in Ireland. Yet by her extortionist policies, her harsh laws against the native Catholics and their religion, and her promotion of a Protestant ruling class, whose major qualification was its compliance with English views, she forfeited any right to be considered equitable, progressive, or humane. The bitterness engendered by the Reformation, the plantations, Cromwell, and the Battle of the Boyne grew during this period of relative calm in Irish affairs to form an indestructible and enduring core of resentment. This resentment was rooted in ethnic, political, religious, and economic bigotry—but a bigotry attributable in large part to those who never were Irish.

It was not until the last decade of the century that trouble started to brew again in Ireland. In 1791, the United Irishmen organization was established in Belfast and Dublin by Wolfe Tone. This group, comprised of Catholics and Presbyterians, supported the twin causes of religious equality and radical political reform. They enjoyed some initial success when restrictions on Catholic education and voting rights were removed in 1793. Eventually, however, the United Irishmen became increasingly extreme in their demands, and in 1798 they joined the French in open rebellion against England. It has been said that their decision to make this alliance with France was prompted by the hope that, if victorious, Ireland would be granted her independence, as the French propagandists had promised. Yet it was this very alliance that doomed the rebellion to ultimate failure. For Ulster Presbyterians, no matter how strongly they disliked the English government, could not finally bring themselves to side with the French in an effort to create an independent Catholic, Celtic Ireland. Ulstermen, therefore, sided with the British, mainly through the agency of the newly founded, militantly anti-Catholic Orange lodges. The rebellion, which was ruthlessly put down, had severe political consequences. The Irish Parliament was abolished, and an appropriate number of members of parliament were integrated into Westminster by the Act of Union (1800).

The union was reluctantly accepted in Ireland. Protestants could see no other way to maintain their dominant position in light of the events that had so strikingly shown their dependence on English aid. Catholics accepted these closer ties with the old enemy, at least in part, because English Prime Minister Pitt promised them a Catholic emancipation bill as part of the union package. To Pitt, union seemed the only way to restore order and justice in Ireland. In the former he succeeded; in the latter he failed. His attempt to have Catholic emancipation added to the Union Act was defeated, for it gained little support in England at the time. Another twenty-eight years were to pass before Catholics were allowed to enter parliament, and the disenchantment and political agitation that occurred during this period contributed to the eventual failure of the union.

1800-1920

As the population of Ireland climbed to about eight million by 1840, their standard of living, dependent on the land, fell. Along with this increasing poverty there was an upsurge in sectarian violence. Members of the Orange Order became more intolerant, especially after passage of the Catholic Emancipation Act of 1829, and Protestant-Catholic animosity was encouraged on both sides by clerical and lay fanatics. One of the first modern religious riots, a forerunner of today's troubles, took place in Belfast in 1835. Two people were shot dead and others injured when soldiers clashed with people celebrating the anniversary of the Battle of the Boyne in Sandy Row—then, as now, a Protestant stronghold. At about the same time, Catholics were wrecking the Protestant area of Smithfield. Serious sectarian riots are also reported to have occurred in 1843, 1849, 1857, 1864, 1872, 1880, 1884, 1886, and 1898.

Andrew Boyd, in his book *Holy War in Belfast*, describes in detail eyewitness accounts of the 1857 riots, which like many others took place during the "marching" season. The following descriptive statements have been taken from his account to show how discouragingly little progress toward community accommodation has been made in 117 years and that, as the Bible indicates, there is nothing new under the sun. All these statements have appeared repeatedly, and in substantially the same form, in our newspapers over the past five years.

- There were emblems and flags (and) sectarian music.
- The mob from Sandy Row were taunting the Catholics and screaming insults about the Pope. The Catholics were equally abusive.
- The aspect of those localities was that of the camp of two armies, waiting only for a convenient time of actual battle.
- Gunmen had barricaded themselves in a nearby house.
- The firing continued every day from these positions, yet the police were unable to capture the gunmen responsible.
- The terrorizing of innocent individuals continued.
- [They] packed their belongings on a handcart and left Stanley Street never to return.
- The council of war decided that . . . the youngest and fittest constables would lay aside their heavy equipment and thus be able to pursue the mobs and make arrests. [These sound like the original snatch squads.]
- [They took] ammunition in the form of paving stones which they prised from the streets.
- The soldiers were hampered by army regulations.
- A special "Inquiry into the Conduct of the Constabulary" was set up.

To return to the general chronology: in 1823, Daniel O'Connell organized the Catholic Association, which sought and achieved Catholic emancipation through Peel and Wellington. Nevertheless, resistance to change was strong, and the implementation of the act was very slow. By 1886, for example, only twelve hundred justices of the peace of a total of five thousand were Catholics. The significance of O'Connell, though, is greater than this political achievement. By helping to change the upper-middle-class Catholic movement into a popular one, featuring clergy and peasantry, he finally and indissolubly cemented together the Catholic Church and Irish nationalism.

The years 1845-55 saw a profound change in the face of Ireland. During the first four years, about one million people died of disease and starvation; another two million emigrated, most of them to the United States. These "lucky" ones took with them a hatred for Britain fanned to a fever pitch by the great famine of 1847, in which a quarter of a million Irish people died of starvation. The cause of the famine was the failure of the potato crop—their main food—and while Britain obviously could not be held responsible for the actual famine, many nevertheless felt that the magnitude of its consequences could have been considerably lessened if the British government had made more help available more quickly. One indirect effect of the famine was to further divide Ulster from the rest of Ireland. People to the north were much less dependent on agriculture than their southern countrymen. They had started a number of industries that were steadily expanding and providing increased wealth in the community. Thus, the impact of the famine was reduced, and Ulstermen did not share to the same degree the general Irish anger toward Britain.

The advent of William Gladstone as British Prime Minister in 1868, with his famous declaration, "My mission is to pacify Ireland," marks another milestone in Irish history. His conversion to the cause of Irish home rule is one of the more remarkable changes that has taken place in modern political history. Yet the actions he took (in his first ministry) indicate that he thought even then that the basis of the union was insecure. And insecure it has proved to be.

In 1868, Gladstone removed one of the major Irish Catholic grievances when he disestablished the Church of Ireland in the face of strong conservative opinion in Britain. His opponents claimed—and they were correct, as it turned out—that such a move would undermine both British and Protestant control in that country. Yet the move was logically defensible. The 1861 census showed that 78% of the population was Catholic, 12% Anglican, and 9% Presbyterian. And although 70% of the Anglicans were in Ulster, even there they constituted a minority. The other main item of Irish legislation in Gladstone's first ministry was the Land Act of 1870, which gave tenant farmers greater security and more clearly defined rights. These had been actively sought since the formation of tenant associations immediately after the famine. The real significance of this act, however, was that it indicated a willingness on the part of the British government to start assuming some of its social responsibilities in Ireland.

The creation of the Home Rule League in 1870 by Isaac Butt, the son of an Anglican minister, returned the whole question of constitutional reform to the forefront of political discussion. The league acted as a channel for nationalist sentiment, and in 1874, fifty-nine Home Rulers, who resolved to act as an independent group, were returned to Westminster. Gladstone attempted to lower the political temperature by introducing in 1881 a second land act designed to strengthen the tenant rights of the Irish peasantry; but this failed. In 1885, eighty-six home rule members were returned to office, and together they held the balance of British legislative power. In return for their parliamentary support, Gladstone introduced the first of his three home rule bills. In each of these bills the concept of Irish independence was strictly limited by the overall supremacy of the Westminster Parliament. What was envisioned by the concept of home rule was little more than glorified local government. Why then were passions so easily aroused? The answer is that everyone thought his particular vested interest was being threatened.

The reasons for English opposition were economic and nationalistic. Ireland was a prime market for English goods and an important source of food supplies, both of which might be threatened by home rule. Even more importantly, conservative England saw in the move a challenge to her territorial integrity. Greeks, Italians, Australians, and Canadians should be, and indeed were, encouraged to manage their own affairs. But no recalcitrant group at home could be allowed to call into question the dominance of England or upset the status quo. So when Lord Randolf Churchill told the people of Larne that "Ulster will fight [against home rule] and Ulster will be right," and when he told the people in Belfast's Ulster Hall that there were many in England who would stand with them regardless of the consequences, he was voicing the opposition of the majority at the time. In Ulster the opposition was political, religious, and economic. The people considered themselves British because of their heritage, and they were unwilling to surrender that privilege. Secondly, they saw in the organization and policy of the home rule movement an identity between Catholicism and nationalism which to them justified the slogan "home rule is Rome rule." Finally, they felt—probably correctly—that any break with Britain would seriously undermine their industries, whose output was directed toward British not Irish markets.

Under the influence of Charles Stewart Parnell, who succeeded Butt and led the Irish M.P.'s at Westminster, the rest of Ireland was initially prepared to accept limited autonomy as a realistic step toward independence. Parnell's achievement of persuading the English Liberals to propose it on the one hand, and of convincing his nationalist colleagues that it was desirable on the other, was considerable. After his death in 1891, however, republican sentiment, fed by the injustices and hatreds of the past, again boiled to the surface, and Ireland was determined to be free.

The first home rule bill was defeated in the House of Commons by a split in the Liberal party's ranks. (The very fact that it was debated at all caused serious disquiet in Ulster and resulted in a great revival of the Orange Order.) The second bill, passed by the Commons but defeated in the Lords, stimulated 12,000 Orangemen from northern constituencies to affirm their total, and if necessary violent, opposition to home rule. By 1912 and the introduction of the third bill, James Craig, later Lord Craigavon, first Prime Minister of Northern Ireland, and Sir Edward Carson, the two leaders of Ulster unionism, were prepared for any eventuality. A provisional Ulster government was established, ready to come into operation on the day that a home rule bill became law. And gun-running took place to the North and South, which the English seemed powerless to stop. On Ulster Day, Sunday, September 28, 1912, after morning religious services, 471,414 Ulster men and women signed a solemn covenant against home rule. Subsequently, an Ulster Volunteer Force (UVF), made up of covenant subscribers, began to drill and march openly in the North in preparation for the expected battle.

In the rest of Ireland two groups competed for public loyalty. The Irish Nationalist party in Westminster, now under the leadership of John Redmond, was still striving for home rule by constitutional means. The second group, started in 1906 and led by Arthur Griffith, was called Sinn Fein ("ourselves alone"). It held that the union with England was illegal and that Irish M.P.'s should withdraw from Westminster and set up an Irish parliament in Dublin. While its influence was not immediately felt, it was certainly responsible, at least in part, for organizing the Irish Volunteers, who became the southern counterpart of the UVF. There was much support in England for the unionists, especially in the Conservative party, and even British statesmen made speeches with violent overtones. Bonar Law, for example, publicly supported the Ulster Volunteers; in 1912 he told a rally in England that he could imagine no lengths of resistance to which Ulster might go that he and, in his belief, an overwhelming majority of the British people would not be prepared to support.

The House of Lords delayed final passage of the bill from 1912 to 1914, during which time Prime Minister Asquith and the King considered excluding Ulster from the bill; but Redmond stoutly resisted. Due to the imminence of war, the act, once passed, was immediately suspended with the agreement of Redmond, Craig, and Carson, who all thought that the conflict with Germany was of more immediate concern. Republican elements in Ireland, however, viewed the war as an ideal opportunity to strike for independence while England was otherwise engaged. Thus, on Easter Monday, 1916, with little public support, Patrick Pearse, James Connolly, and Joseph Plunkett led an uprising in Dublin, and from the captured General Post Office declared Ireland a republic. The rebellion failed, many were hurt in the ensuing skirmishes, and hundreds were arrested. Fifteen of the leaders were tried and executed, though one of them, Eamonn DeValera, the now-retired Irish President, was merely imprisoned; he had influential American friends who exerted pressure on the British government in his behalf. To the British the uprising was simply an act of treason that had to be dealt with promptly and ruthlessly. To the Irish, not even its romantic absurdity could quench the spark of hope and anticipation that it briefly ignited. James Connolly said, "Never had man or woman a grander cause, never was a cause more grandly served." And despite its magnificent failure, many Irishmen began to agree with him.

In the two years following the Anglo-German war, attitudes in the North and South hardened still further. Those in the North contrasted their military service in the armed forces with the treasonable actions of Sinn Fein and renewed their anti-home rule vows. In the South, Griffith and Michael Collins trained and organized anti-British terrorists, while DeValera went on a propaganda and fund-raising trip to America. The pressure of violence finally led the British government to declare illegal both Sinn Fein and the "Irish government" meeting in the Dial in Dublin. The latter was formed by the seventy-three Sinn Fein candidates who were elected to Westminster in the 1918 election but refused to take their seats there.

The upshot of all this was "the troubles." The Irish Republican Army (IRA), the military wing of Sinn Fein, began a brutal campaign against the police and government troops. These latter, the Black and Tans, were a special force of British ex-servicemen who owed their name to the black belts and khaki uniforms they wore. This savage guerilla war, which raged from 1920-22, was characterized by atrocities and reprisals on both sides. In Ulster alone, nearly three hundred people were killed, many of them in Belfast. At the same time, there was considerable pressure on both sides to find an acceptable end to the conflict. Foreign opinion, especially American opinion, was strongly against the British, who to them appeared to be coercing a people seeking self-determination.

But the IRA also had its problems. Even after its policy was formally adopted by DeValera on behalf of the Dial in 1921, it still suffered from all the characteristic difficulties of insurgents: lack of money, ammunition, and manpower. Thus, the situation was a stalemate. Britain could win the war militarily, but to do so would mean abandoning political influence. The IRA could not win militarily but had the support of the people.

The compromise solution came in two parts. In 1920, the Government of Ireland Act provided for two Irish parliaments: the one in Belfast was to govern Antrim, Down, Tyrone, Fermanagh, Armagh, and Londonderry; the parliament in Dublin was to govern the rest of the country. The authority of the northern parliament, which was opened by George V, was initially rejected by Ulster's Catholic population. To suspicious unionist minds this indicated collusion with the terrorists of the South, and the new province got off to a bad start from which it has never recovered. In the South, all the elected Sinn Fein members boycotted the Dublin parliament, and eventually "independence" negotiations started between Lloyd George of England and Arthur Griffith and Michael Collins of Ireland. The resulting "treaty," signed on December 6, 1921, gave Ireland independent dominion status within the British Commonwealth. In fact, it was similar to the 1914 Home Rule Act. The treaty included three provisions, however, which the Irish found distasteful and on which DeValera based his opposition to it. These were: an oath of allegiance to the British crown as befitted Commonwealth subjects, the freedom of Northern Ireland to withdraw from the newly created state and remain within the United Kingdom, and the retention by Britain of certain Irish naval bases. The treaty was finally approved by the Dial, and a provisional government under Michael Collins was set up in January 1922. Perhaps it is a commentary on the strength of nationalist feeling on both sides of the

Irish Sea that within a year of the treaty signing, Lloyd George was out of office, Griffith had died, and Collins had been murdered.

SINCE 1921

The division of Ireland became the main bone of contention in both North and South once the two governments took office. Although the election in June 1922 produced in Dublin a pro-treaty majority, the country was deeply divided on the treaty, and a form of civil war broke out soon afterwards. The new government took over the anti-IRA role that had been relinquished by the British, while political opposition to the settlement was led by DeValera. However, the IRA commanded decreasing support among the people, and DeValera finally announced the end of resistance in 1923. Intermittent violence continued, but it became even more isolated when DeValera and his followers took the oath of allegiance and assumed their place in the Dial in 1927. By this time Collins had been succeeded by W.T. Cosgrave, whose administration laid the foundation of Ireland's political philosophy, one that remains substantially unaltered to this day. Politically, she has sought to emphasize her sovereign independence, including her desire to see a united Ireland. Successive governments have tried to support an attractive and diversified industrial policy so that the country might attain both greater wealth and a greater degree of economic independence from Britain. Culturally, Ireland has stressed her "Irishness."

DeValera, who was prime minister from 1932 to 1948, continued these general policies but did not feel bound by the provisions of the treaty he had opposed. Early in his administration he abolished the oath of allegiance and from 1936-38 produced a new constitution that made the country a republic in everything but name. In fact, the degree of separation from Britain was underscored by the neutral stance that his government took during the Second World War. J.A. Costello, who followed him in 1948, completed the separation by proclaiming Ireland a republic on Easter Monday, 1949. In that same year Westminster passed the Ireland Act, which established two constitutional points of great importance. The first was that the constitutional position of Northern Ireland could not be changed without the consent of the Northern Ireland Parliament at Stormont. (Today this is usually expressed in the phrase "without the consent of the majority.") The second was that the imperial government could not intervene in Ulster's internal affairs unless a breakdown in law and order occurred. This was the basis of the Downing Street Declaration of August 1969, which dispatched British troops to quell the Belfast riots.

In Ulster, Craigavon quickly accepted partition as the salvation of Northern Ireland, and unionists pointed to the civil war in the South to illustrate their completely different attitudes toward Britain. Belfast's policy was to increase its British links and to maintain the Protestant ascendancy by whatever means necessary. Craigavon, who governed until 1940, said in 1934: "I have always said I am an Orangeman first and a politician and a member of this parliament afterwards . . . all I boast is that we are a Protestant parliament and a Protestant State." And Craigavon's successor, Sir Basil Brooke (later Lord Brookeborough), who was prime minister until 1963, urged: "There are a great number of Protestants and Orangemen who employ Roman Catholics. . . . I would appeal to loyalists, whenever possible, to employ good Protestant lads and lassies." Eight months later, referring to this statement, he said: "Thinking out the whole question carefully . . . I recommend those people who are loyalists not to employ Roman Catholics, ninety-nine per cent of whom are disloyal. . . ."

Terence O'Neill, though from a background similar to that of his predecessor, at least tried to establish a working relationship with the South. To this end he met with Sean Lemass, the Irish Prime Minister, in both Belfast and Dublin during 1965. These meetings took place at a time of reduced tension both between North and South—after the abortive IRA terror campaign of the fifties had ended —and between the two communities in Northern Ireland. Nevertheless, they immediately provoked protest. Rightwing unionists interpreted them as the beginning of a rapprochement that would eventually undermine their monopoly of power. Catholics, though always pleased to have increased good will, really wanted substantial reforms and saw in the talks a chance to achieve them.

Early opposition to the more liberal attitudes introduced by O'Neill was spearheaded by an evangelical minister, Rev. Ian R.K. Paisley. He construed the government's policies in religious terms as a move toward an accommodation with Roman Catholicism, and in political terms as a betrayal of the province's historical heritage; thus he acted as a vociferous spokesman for many Protestants. His threat to lead his followers into the Catholic Divis Street area of Belfast to remove a tricolor (the Irish flag, whose display is illegal in Northern Ireland) flying above the republicans' headquarters during the election campaign of 1964 forced the Home Affairs minister at Stormont to order the police to do the job instead. The republicans and their sympathizers reacted violently, and the ensuing riots had a significance far beyond the immediate threat to life and property. First, because they took place during an election campaign, they were given immense press and television coverage all over the world. People were thus forcibly reminded of the undercurrents of bitterness that are an integral part of Ulster society. Secondly, the violence redivided that society into two antagonistic camps with a rigidity that had been missing since the early days of the province. Thirdly, the riots signaled the beginning of the end of uninterrupted Unionist dominance. After this, people started to make their own voices heard through spokesmen for new political and special interest groups. It was almost as if they were claiming that all the major political parties were an irrelevance at the grass-roots level.

Two of these new groupings were the Ulster Volunteer Force (UVF) and the Civil Rights Association (CRA). The former was an extreme right-wing Protestant group, which declared war on the IRA in the summer of 1966. After four Catholics were shot by its members on Malvern Street in 1968, O'Neill placed the UVF alongside the IRA

The Civil Rights Association, formed by students at Queens University in Belfast in the late sixties, used protesting demonstrations similar to those of the American student movement of the early sixties. These civil rights marchers in Londonderry, mainly Roman Catholic students demanding equality in jobs, housing, and votes for Northern Ireland's Catholics, were halted by police to prevent them from clashing with Ulster loyalist extremists.

on the outlawed list. This, of course, further outraged
loyalist Protestant opinion. The Civil Rights Association
was organized in February 1967, with a five-fold objective. It sought:

  (i)   to define the basic rights of all citizens;
  (ii) to protect the rights of the individual;
  (iii) to highlight all possible abuses of power;
  (iv) to demand guarantees for freedom of speech, as-
        sembly and association;
  (v)   to inform the public of their lawful rights.

Initially such lofty intentions drew support from both
Protestants and Catholics. But by 1968 these principles
had been translated into a much more practical form. The
civil rights movement was by then pursuing, more militantly: universal franchise at the local level; the redrawing of local election boundaries; legislation to outlaw discrimination in local government; a points system for the
allocation of council houses; and the repeal of the Special
Powers Act. The particular stigma of the latter was that
it included the right of the government to intern people
without trial.

To most Protestants these pursuits proved that the CRA
had abandoned its democratic ideals and had descended
to religio-political warfare. They felt that this program
was in effect challenging the very existence of the state
by trying to change the well-tried formulas of government.
Before long, the CRA had become largely Catholic, and its
associations with People's Democracy, a radical student
group based at Queens University that kept up a pressure
of demonstrations and demands on Stormont, further
alienated conservative unionists. The inevitable clashes
began between these conservative unionists, radical
Catholics, republicans, and the police. The two worst
took place in Derry in October 1968, when police clashed
with CRA marchers, and at Burntollet in January 1969,
when all four parties were involved. In fact, the violent

Each July, thousands of Orangemen parade throughout Ulster to commemorate the victory of Protestant King William of Orange over Catholic ex-King James at the Battle of Boyne in 1690. The Belfast parade is the largest and can take two and one half hours to pass a given spot.

behavior of the police in Derry was thought by some to be the incident that started the deterioration in law and order that finally led to the downfall of O'Neill's government. Also, at about that time Paisley was sent to jail for his part in an assault on news media personnel in Armagh during the previous November.

In April, Bernadette Devlin, a twenty-two-year-old radical student and leader of the CRA, won a parliamentary bye-election and, by making a pungent maiden speech on behalf of "the minority" only minutes after being sworn in at Westminster, acquired world-wide exposure for Catholic demands. One week later, O'Neill, having lost Unionist support, resigned and was succeeded by his distant cousin Chichester-Clark. The latter continued the policies of reform and on May 6th ordered all prosecutions against civil rights leaders and militant Protestants dropped in an attempt to improve community feeling.

The Orange celebrations on the 12th of July, 1969 were marked by passionate outbursts in both speech and action. At Castlereagh, Paisley told assembled Orangemen that they were engaged in "the great battle of Biblical Protestantism against popery." The Prime Minister, at Moneymore, depicted Irish republicans as murderers. And rioting occurred in the streets of Belfast, Lurgan, Derry, and Dungiven. By early August, Paisleyites, Catholics, and police were clashing with greater violence and an increasing disregard for life and property. Finally, the Apprentice Boys march and actions in Derry on August 12th so provoked that city's Catholics that they attacked the marchers and later the police. Two days of bloody warfare followed before the police were able to "retake" the Bogside area in which the Catholics had barricaded themselves. People everywhere in the province were terror-stricken, intimidated, and vulnerable to attack, and Northern Ireland was on the verge of civil war.

It can be said that civil war started in Belfast on the

14th. That night extremists of both sides and B-specials, an auxiliary—largely Protestant—police force, went on a spree of shooting and arson that claimed eight lives. The spectacle of Bombay Street, between the Protestant Shankill and Catholic Falls Roads, burning from end to end, signaled the total inability of Stormont to enforce law and order or to protect the citizenry. Consequently, the British government had to step in, and Prime Minister Wilson sent six thousand officers and men into West Belfast to restore order. Thus, Britain, after a physical absence of less than fifty years, was again directly involved in the affairs of Ireland.

2 THE BURDEN OF NORTHERN IRELAND AND ITS MEANING FOR AMERICA

THE TRAGIC EVENTS unfolding in Northern Ireland, reported so relentlessly by the news media in recent years, have become a burden on the consciences of thoughtful people everywhere. This is especially true in North America, where there are millions of persons of British and Irish descent. Accurate information is often difficult to obtain, and most people realize that it is not as simple as the partisan sloganeers would have it: the conflict is far more complex than "law and order versus criminal anarchy" or "liberation and justice versus the degradation of a subject people." To Christians the burden is all the greater because the principals in the conflict continue to echo the slogans of the Reformation—slogans that shame all of us when shouted over barricades amid the sounds of rifle fire, or when whispered by small groups of men and women alongside a lonely Irish road while waiting to commit the next act of sectarian violence against an approaching victim. The burden imposed by the events in Northern Ireland requires the understanding and sympathy of those of us who are vitally interested and involved because of ethnic heritage and/or religious conviction. If for no other reasons, we are all involved in Northern Ireland because we are human beings and because humanity is being violated as long as the violent and brutal struggle continues. The bells of both Protestant and Catholic churches toll nearly every day in Ulster for the ever-mounting number of victims of "the troubles." We should "ask not for whom the bell tolls," for we are all involved in Northern Ireland.

The body of baby Angela Gallagher, the victim of a terrorist's bullet, is carried to the cemetery in the arms of her father, adding poignancy to the real tragedy of Northern Ireland.

I

It is not surprising that Northern Ireland is being debated by people in North America when one recalls that the United States and Canada are at the center of a North Atlantic community that was internationalized by the folk-migrations of the nineteenth century. Surely one of the most important themes of modern history is the migration of some 55 million people from Europe, approximately 37.5 million of whom came to the United States and Canada (33 million and 4.5 million respectively). Migrants to the New World brought with them the talents and expectations that have helped to create the strength and vitality of North American culture; but, as part of their cultural baggage, they also brought with them the mentalities and ideologies of the nations and peoples from which they came. Although most migrants were assimilated, in varying degrees, in their adopted lands, it was understandable that they wished to maintain contacts with their homelands through various channels of kinship and friendship. The United States, and to a lesser extent Canada, assumed some of the problems of the Old World—political, religious, and ethnic—when it received "the huddled masses yearning to breathe free." The animosities of Europe were partially transferred to our shores, and the continuing difficulties in Europe and elsewhere have been followed with great interest because of the contacts North Americans have maintained with those still "at home." In many cases this interest has taken the form of a fraternal association that sought to maintain cultural or linguistic links with the traditional heritage. Less frequently, but with potential explosiveness, this interest has become so intense as to demand recognition in American foreign policy.

The most obviously explosive example is the policy of the United States towards the Middle East. One may applaud the present policy of American support for Israel, and one may like to think that this policy, without which Israel probably could not survive, was based on principle. But it would be less than realistic to believe that our policy was conceived and followed without regard to domestic realities. The plain fact is that the United States population contains a large number of Jews and relatively few Arabs. The Jews, furthermore, constitute a visible and articulate minority who are grouped in electorally sensitive states, and politicians are often receptive to their requests or demands. One wonders what our Middle East policy would be, especially in view of the Arab control of so much of the world's available oil, if the relative numbers of Jewish and Arab immigrants had been reversed. It seems fairly clear that present American sympathies would be placed differently had the historic force of migration brought a different mix of Semitic peoples to the United States.

Similarly, Americans over forty will remember the internal social dislocations that occurred in this country during, and because of, World War II. With the rise of fascism in Italy and Germany we saw the concomitant rise of organizations in America seeking to emulate the "new order" in the fatherlands. The Germans were the best organized, and many persons of German-American ancestry marched under the banner of Fritz Kuhn's *Bund*. Less well-organized, but highly visible and vocal, were the efforts aimed at generating support for the Mussolini regime among persons of Italian-American ancestry. Ironically, Japanese-Americans were never very active in supporting the Japanese brand of fascism, but they were nevertheless victims of relocation in the hysterical aftermath of Pearl Harbor. The United States, precisely because it opened its doors to the restless and expectant peoples of the world, created within itself a forum in which its citizens sought not only to settle their own problems but also to settle, or at least become involved in, the problems of the rest of the world.

Historically, one of the most important connections between the United States and Europe has been the intrusion of the problems of Ireland on the American scene. One reason is that the Irish have been one of the most numerous and important immigrant groups. Because of agricultural disasters, overpopulation, an exploitative land-tenure system, and religious strife, the Irish came to the United States in millions. Due to a phenomenal natural increase, as well as continual accessions from the old country, Irish-Americans comprise one of the largest numerical minority groups in the country.

Irish immigration came in two waves. The first, mostly during the eighteenth and early nineteenth centuries, was overwhelmingly Protestant. They are known as Scots-Irish, but the inserted reference to a Scottish background has less to do with nationality than religion: "Scots-Irish" should be understood as Protestant Irish. Many of them were from Dissenter (Presbyterian) backgrounds; their ancestors had emigrated from Scotland to Ireland in the previous century to escape religious oppression. The descendants, finding themselves under similar disabilities because of the ascendancy of the Church of Ireland (Anglican), continued the quest for a place to practice their religion freely by migrating to the United States. These Protestant Irish seldom remained in the eastern cities of America; they typically moved to farm areas along the then-western edge of the frontier. They usually had some capital or brought farm implements with them, and they were able to establish communities in what is today western Pennsylvania, West Virginia, western Maryland and Virginia, eastern Tennessee and Kentucky, and western North Carolina. They played an important part in the American Revolution, not only because they occupied the sensitive frontier settlements, but also because they hoped that the Revolution would result in the disestablishment of the Church of England in several colonies.

If the Protestant Irish migration was a wave, the Roman Catholic Irish migration was a tidal wave, and it reached truly gigantic proportions during the middle third of the nineteenth century. Because their Protestant countrymen were called "Scots-Irish" in America, the Roman Catholics were known simply as "the Irish"—a linkage that acquired tragic dimensions, prefiguring a later development in Irish consciousness in which to be Catholic was to be Irish, but to be Protestant was to be British. The Protestants, mostly in the north of Ireland, chose to migrate to America because they wanted to live in an environment that afforded greater economic and religious freedom. The Catholics had no such luxury of choice. They did not choose America as such: migration was not an option freely exercised—it was the last resort in the efforts of a people to survive. Mostly from the south of Ireland, and especially from the still underdeveloped southwest, the Catholics had been driven to the wall, partly because of overpopulation, but mostly because of an exploitative land policy carried out in the name of absentee English landlords. Their impoverished diet had been reduced to a literal dependence on the potato. The blight on the potato crop during the 1840s and 1850s caused a famine, which left only two choices open to many Catholics—migration or starvation. For those who were still able to eke out a living at home, the political climate was also blighted by the demise of the democratic movement led by the powerful but nonviolent Daniel O'Connell, and by his death in 1847.

The transit to, and initial reception in, North America was a continuation of the tragic history of the Irish emigrants. Possessing very little money, they typically booked their passage on the ships charging the lowest fares, so they had to content themselves with appalling conditions aboard ship. Emigrant ships usually took both saloon (first-class) passengers and steerage (ordinary) passengers. The conditions in the steerage of emigrant ships varied enormously. Many of the Irish who came during the flood tide of migration endured the worst of these conditions. The crowding and the lack of privacy or washing facilities on some ships were rivaled only in the infamous "middle passage" which slaves had endured when they were being transported from Africa. As to food, the slaves may well have fared better in some instances, if for no more noble reason than the economic advantage of bringing healthy slaves to New Orleans or Charleston. The ship owners who brought the Irish to Boston, New York, or Quebec had no such incentive: the passage had been paid in advance. Deaths aboard ship were common, and if a contagious disease broke out, the death toll often rose to one-half the approximately 400 passengers, as was reported in several instances.

Those who survived the journey and arrived in good health faced immediate problems of finding a means of livelihood. Some were fortunate enough to have relatives in North America, who may well have paid the passage for the emigrant. But in most cases, even if a relative was there to receive them, there was often little extra room or food for the new arrivals. Many Irishmen could not afford the passage all the way to the United States, even if that is where they wanted to go. Thousands used all their money to book passages as far as St. John's, Newfoundland, Halifax, Nova Scotia, or St. John, New Brunswick. In some cases they remained in their new homes, but many of them eventually continued their journey to the United States. The most popular Canadian destination for the poor emigrants was Quebec, simply because it was the furthest point in North America to which their money could take them. Few remained in Quebec or Montreal, despite Catholic predominance there; this was perhaps due both to linguistic difficulties and an aversion to settle in any domain still under British rule.

Unlike the Protestant Irish of the earlier migration, the Catholics brought little money with them, which is understandable enough given the circumstances of their migration; but this simple fact had a great deal to do with their pattern of settlement and their adjustment to and acculturation in the United States. Despite Horace Greeley's injunction to go west, few young Irishmen did. Although land on the frontier was either cheap or free, one needed a certain amount of money to finance both the trip west and the beginnings of a settlement. Another deterrent to going west was the fluidity of the ecclesiastical situation on the frontier. The harsh truth is that the perception of Christianity by the Catholic Irish was severely circumscribed by their clergy, who, perhaps with good intentions, herded their followers together into parishes in the eastern cities. Preying upon the simplicity and ignorance of the common people, the priests often created the "state of siege" mentality within which the Irish were content to live in their miserable ghetto communities. The young, intent on trying their luck on the frontier, were dissuaded from doing so by the priest, who portrayed the horrors of being cut off from the church, which alone was the guardian of the means of grace. Many people did go west, of course, and they were soon followed, or preceded, by a dedicated and courageous clergy; but most Irish migrants stayed in or near the city in which they first landed. Their descendants often remained also, thus accounting for the large Irish proportion of the population in such cities as Boston, Providence, New York, Philadelphia, and Baltimore.

Because conditions in Ireland were so desperate, the highest priority for the newly arrived immigrant was usually saving enough money to pay for the passage of the next member or members of the family. The conditions at home required the dismembering of families and may well have contributed to the development of clannishness in Irish families in America; once together again, they would abide no more separations. A young man might have been selected to go first; he would hope to find a well-paying job while he kept his personal expenses low by taking his meals and a room with a cousin who had gone to Boston the year before. In the course of time the family could hope for prepaid tickets to America. Young girls often went alone to work as servants, but few of them entertained hopes of earning enough money to bring anyone else. Their main reason for going may have been that once gone they would no longer be a drain on the already overburdened resources of the family. In the middle nineteenth century the common assumption was that nearly every Catholic family in Ireland had a member in America. Whether or not that was statistically accurate, it suggests the fundamental wrenching of the Irish family because of emigration. To be Irish was to know the pain of being separated from loved ones, not always by choice, but often of necessity. The heartbreak of enforced estrangement was part of Irish life, both in Ireland and America; this was doubly poignant for a people predisposed to melancholy and sentiment. The Irish-American folk song "The Leaving of Liverpool" suggests the feeling. It begins with hope and self-confidence:

> Fare thee well, my own true love,
> When I return, united we will be,
> It's not the leaving of Liverpool that grieves me,
> But my darling when I think of thee.

But the last verse recognizes that in all probability this is not farewell but good-bye:

> *The sun is on the harbour, love,*
> *And I wish I could remain,*
> *But I know it will be a long, long time*
> *Before I see you again.*

The economic conditions that the Irish found in America were scarcely more promising than those they had left in Ireland. Economically viewed, the Irish were a "surplus labor pool" that enabled industry in New England to go through the initial stages of economic growth. For industry to grow at this stage, profits had to be plowed back into capital expansion. Profits, of course, can be attained by several means, including charging high prices for the products manufactured or paying low wages to the workers in the industry. In the initial stages of growth, New England industrialists, especially in textiles, were reluctant to raise prices unduly because this would have eroded their competitive advantage in the domestic American market in relation to English goods. However, the other option for maximizing profits could be employed because of the overabundance of unskilled Irish labor in eastern New England. In the days before the successful organization of labor unions, the surplus labor pool was tapped very cunningly by the manufacturers, and the profits rolled in.

The industrial exploitation of the Irish paralleled the plantation exploitation of the slaves. Both in providing a commodity for foreign exchange and in providing a raw material for domestic manufacturing, the "cotton kingdom," built on slavery, was the vital first step in the great economic growth of the United States. The second step in economic growth came in the Northeast. The unskilled workers, a majority of whom were Irish, were caught in an economic system that stopped short of slavery but left the Irish workers nonetheless in a vicious circle of poverty and dependence. Indeed, despite the "monstrous injustice" of the institution of slavery, the slave may have been better off in terms of daily subsistence. He seldom wanted for food and shelter, and his relatively good treat-. ment was a necessity for his master, if for no other reason than to protect his investment (the value of prime field-hands rose threefold between 1830 and 1860). The personal welfare of the industrial worker was not the responsibility of his employer, and if one fell by the wayside, there was another to take his place.

The social climate that greeted the Irish in the United States was nearly as harsh as the economic conditions they encountered. Despite the fact that the Irish were welcomed as cheap labor by the employers, other segments of the "native" population, especially in New England, were opposed to Irish immigration. The economic threat of surplus labor gave tangible shape to the wild stories and fears that excited the Protestant population. Ethno-religious descrimination was so blatant in New England that job advertisements would frequently say, "No Irish Need Apply"; such discrimination was practiced openly until well into the twentieth century. The presence of large numbers of Catholics in America was a threat to the belief held by many Americans, particularly in New England, that the United States was a Protestant country. This country, the belief assumed, was "the world's last best hope," and one needed to pledge one hundred percent allegiance to it in order to be a full citizen. This immediately excluded all "Romanists" because of their subservience to the pope of Rome, who was the head of a foreign state. Protestant critics were fond of quoting Jesus' words, "You cannot serve two masters." The anti-Catholic sentiment found its most pointed political expression in the "Know-Nothing" party in the northeastern states during the time of heaviest Irish migration. This sentiment drove the Irish into the willing arms of the Democrats, who later would build their majority in many states on the basis of immigrant support. Until very recently, in most of New England the almost irrevocable rule of politics allied the Protestants and Republicans against the Catholics and Democrats. As late as 1928, the Democratic nominee for President, Alfred E. Smith, was opposed by Herbert C. Hoover, who ran victoriously, at least in part, on a sentiment that would unite Protestant America in opposition to a "Catholic in the White House."

In the decades following the Civil War, and especially in the twentieth century, the descendants of Irish immigrants grew in political strength and sophistication. Long before "Black Power" was suggested by militant blacks, "Irish Power" was being practiced successfully in many cities by leaders such as John "Honey-Fitz" Fitzgerald, the grandfather of John Fitzgerald Kennedy. As Irish political strength grew, politicians became more sensitive to Irishmen's needs. Not only did the Irish demand domestic redress of grievance, they also demanded that the United States do something either to help Ireland gain its independence from Britain, or to persuade Britain to act more beneficently toward Ireland—especially toward its Catholic population. In several foreign policy questions the United States appeared to reflect the anti-British Fenian attitude of Irish nationalists who had become expatriates in the United States. During the Civil War, when a group of Fenians invaded Canada in a vain attempt to link once again the slaves with the Irish in a common desire for emancipation, the general attitude of "twisting the British lion's tail" almost caused open hostilities.

Given the large number of Americans of Irish descent and their political acumen, as well as their belief that Ireland's tragic history has been largely a story of British-Protestant exploitation, it is understandable that Irish-Americans have remained concerned and involved in the problems of Ireland. First it was independence, and more recently it has been the unification of the dismembered state. Those who migrated lost none of the dimension of feeling for the exploitation of the Irish. Because of their unhappy history in Ireland under British rule and their scarcely less unhappy history in America, Irish-Americans tend to link Protestantism with exploitation, both in Ireland and the United States. Now that Irish-Americans as a group have overcome through political power their economic and social disabilities in America, and in view of the independence of the Republic of Ireland, their most poignant concern is for the Catholic minority in Northern Ireland, who allegedly remain second-class citizens. The Irish-Americans who speak out against British policy in Ulster do not view themselves as foreign nationals interfering in the domestic affairs of a friendly state, but as participants in the final phase of the struggle of Celtic, Roman Catholic peoples to free themselves, at long last, from the domination of Anglo-Saxon, Protestant peoples.

II

President John F. Kennedy was a personal link between the Irish of the new and old worlds. He has been viewed by Catholics in Ireland, both in the Republic and in Ulster, as "one of us who made it" in the Protestant-dominated, Anglo-Saxon, North Atlantic culture. Kennedy's constituency included more than Massachusetts or even the United States; it extended across the Atlantic to the "Emerald Isle" because of innumerable personal ties that Irish people have created and maintained over the centuries. Whereas Northern Ireland Protestants might have a picture of Queen Elizabeth and the Duke of Edinburgh in their homes, Catholics usually have pictures of either John Kennedy or the Kennedy brothers, and their popularity is exceeded only by that of the ubiquitous Virgin Mary. Edward M. Kennedy, the sole survivor of that family, is heir to the tradition that began with his brothers. He has inherited the Irish-American constituency and with it the responsibility of being one of its principal spokesmen. For that constituency the main issue remains the same: justice for Irish Catholics, especially in Northern Ireland, and justice can only obtain when Ireland is reunited.

Senator Kennedy recently has made the most comprehensive statement by a leading American politician on the problem of Northern Ireland ("Ulster is an International Issue," *Foreign Policy*, Summer, 1973; reprinted in abridged form in *The London Times*, 31 May, 1973, as "Why Unity is the only Path to Peace in Ireland"). His ideas deserve careful attention because they may well represent the thinking of a majority of Irish-Americans. It is the view of the present writers that, while some of Senator Kennedy's ideas are both helpful and deserving of public acceptance in the United States, many others are neither helpful nor deserving of public acceptance with a view toward making them American public policy toward Ireland and Britain. If this review of the Senator's ideas is largely unfavorable, it is not because the authors have a particular axe to grind in favor of one side or the other in the current problems of Northern Ireland, nor between Republicans and Democrats in the United States; rather, it is because we respect the Senator enough to express publicly our doubts about his suggestions for a solution in Northern Ireland, and to question the wisdom of his insistence on American participation in the solution, however wise or just that solution may be.

As was noted in the previous chapter, one must concede at the outset the substantial accuracy of Senator Kennedy's assertion that the Catholics of Northern Ireland have been historic victims of political, social, and economic discrimination. One must also concede the substantial accuracy of his allegation that a principal root of the recent troubles was the historic reluctance of British leaders at Westminster and Protestant leaders in the Northern Ireland Parliament at Stormont to act decisively in behalf of the legitimate demands of the Catholic minority; however, encouraging momentum in this direction from Westminster can now be seen.

Having correctly suggested that social injustice toward Catholics exists in Northern Ireland, Senator Kennedy goes on to suggest that social justice will not really obtain unless and until the six counties in Northern Ireland are reunited with the twenty-six counties in the Republic. Whether or not he is correct in this, there are many problems along the way to be considered before such a hope can be realized. The principal problem is that the constitutional position of Northern Ireland as a part of the United Kingdom is clearly established and that no constitutional changes can occur without the consent of the people of Northern Ireland. Since the Protestant majority wants to maintain the status quo, the advocates of change must necessarily discuss the constitutional issue in a larger context. What is at stake is the historic principle of self-determination—a cardinal tenet of Western democratic faith. But the concept of "the self-determination of all peoples," in defense of which the United States has gone to war several times, is a concept that is more difficult to apply in certain circumstances than at first it might appear.

In March 1973, a plebiscite was held on the constitutional issue, in which the voters of Northern Ireland were asked to respond to two questions: Should Northern Ireland remain a part of the United Kingdom? should Northern Ireland become a part of the Republic of Ireland? Given the electoral majority of the Protestants, it was predictable that the vote would result—as it did—in an overwhelming endorsement of the status quo. This is the nub of the constitutional issue: since partition in 1920 was a regional adjustment to the divisions in Ireland, and the people of Ulster were promised that their constitutional position would not be changed without their consent, it is extremely difficult to know how one can demand a change in the rules at so late a date. Kennedy comes to the attack frontally and questions the entire notion of how one understands the "self-determination of all peoples." To Kennedy, Northern Ireland is not "a state," and Ulstermen are not "a people" as such; to grant them self-determination "is a travesty of a noble principle." The Irish people, Kennedy apparently believes, are one people (which can be shown to be erroneous), and any political divisions between them must be regarded as temporary and illegitimate. Kennedy's words become venomous when discussing Ulster: Northern Ireland is neither a state nor a province but an "uncouth entity that Britain spawned in 1920"; Britain sought to perpetuate it by abusing the noble concept of self-determination because it knew that "the calculated and cynical gerrymander that produced Ulster 50 years ago" would always return Protestant (and British) majorities. Kennedy asks an important question: "If there is to be self-determination for Ulster, why not self-determination for Londonderry, or County Tyrone or any other predominantly Catholic area in Ulster?" The matter of how one can and should configure "a state" or "a people" so that they can determine their own future is a subject that deserves serious consideration.

The fact is that a state or a people is usually configured on the basis of what is likely to benefit the outcome which the determining nation desires. This was seen in Indo-China: those who wanted "Vietnam for the Vietnamese" opposed American policy because they believed that the people of Vietnam were one, notwithstanding the temporary division of the nation in 1954; those who supported American policy suggested that the South Vietnamese were "a people" whose right to self-determination was

Ireland

being interfered with by the aggression of an "outside power," representing another "people." In short, no real debate on the constitutional aspects of self-determination ever really took place in the context of Indo-China because critics or supporters of various wartime administrations chose their positions more with an eye to political realities than constitutional scruples. Whether or not one would apply Kennedy's term for Ulster ("uncouth entity") to South Vietnam tells a great deal about one's thoughts regarding the events there during the past decade. The basic constitutional question is: must the larger entity always prevail over the smaller entity? This complements a basic sociological question: when and how does a group of persons become different enough to desire a future for their own community separated from the larger community?

North Americans need go no further than their own history to understand the difficulty of the problem. Canadians know well the uneasiness with which they viewed the United States, especially during the nineteenth century, when the jingoists were shouting manifest destiny slogans. The American expansionists believed that it was the destiny of the United States to bring the entire North American continent under its domain. What would have occurred if a North American plebiscite had been held? Is there any doubt that the North American "people" would have opted for continental unity? In the actual event, the "people" of Canada rejected American overtures for annexation; it was a case of the smaller prevailing over the larger. In another Canadian instance— the French-speaking population of Quebec—the reverse has been true, and the larger has prevailed over the smaller. Surely, if ever a case for separate identity existed, it is the case of the Quebecois, who were forced by conquest to unite with English-speaking British North America. In both of these Canadian cases one may argue that more justice has resulted because of the way events turned out; but one can easily imagine another set of definitions for "nation" and "people" that would result in different conclusions in both cases.

In the United States, the most traumatic episode in its history—the Civil War—focused the questions of "nation" and "people"; but once again the questions were not settled constitutionally but militarily. Because the South lost the war, the constitutional issues raised by Confederate political philosophers have been lost sight of in American political debates during the ensuing years. For our present purposes, it may be worthwhile to review briefly the principles that moved the Confederate leaders to secede, because it may give us another perspective with which to view the constitutional problem of Northern Ireland.

The issue of states' rights versus federal authority has been debated throughout American history. It was present in the first constitutional document of the nation, the Articles of Confederation, which conceived of effective power residing with the state governments rather than with the national government. The conservatives who wrote the Constitution in 1787, however, vested far more power in the national government; but even they had to compromise with states' rights advocates on several important matters. Southerners have raised the issue many times because of their belief that the national government, while possibly reflecting the sentiments of a majority of Americans, did not reflect the sentiments of a majority of (white) people in their region. The immediate issues that have caused Southerners to protest what they have regarded as the abuse of power by the national government have varied in the past 180 years: Thomas Jefferson and James Madison led the states' rights cause with the Virginia and Kentucky Resolutions (1798), because they believed that the administration of John Adams had usurped and abused power in the matter of civil liberties when it passed the Alien and Sedition Laws; John C. Calhoun led the states' rights cause in 1828 against Andrew Jackson's administration because of his belief that the government's tariff policy was ruinous to the economy of the South; Jefferson Davis, Alexander Stephens, and others moved the states' rights position its next logical step in 1861, when the Southern Confederacy removed itself from the Union in opposition to what it saw as the Lincoln administration's position on slavery, the region's "peculiar institution"; in more recent history, Governors Faubus and Wallace have raised the standard of states' rights against the Eisenhower and Kennedy administrations, respectively, on the matter of federally directed school integration. In each of these examples, the issue was resolved, in varying degrees, by a victory for the advocates of federal authority. Indeed, the institutional history of American politics has been largely the story of a federal government that has continually expanded its powers at the expense of the states, and, within the federal government itself, of a presidency that has continually expanded its powers at the expense of the other branches. This process has done violence to the intentions of the founding fathers, who viewed good government as the result of a delicate balance between the various branches on local, state, and federal levels. If balanced government could be maintained, the fathers believed, their two goals would be realized: the will of the majority would prevail in most cases; but, of equal importance, the rights of a minority interest would be safeguarded.

The most important American political philosopher whose life and work was the defense of a minority interest was John C. Calhoun of South Carolina. While nearly all students of American politics would agree with Richard Hofstadter's view that Calhoun was "the last American statesman to do any primary political thinking," most give little attention to Calhoun because his views are associated with the political heresy of secession and the moral outrage of slavery. Calhoun's biographer, Charles M. Wiltse, sees him as "the supreme champion of minority rights" (however, it should perhaps be noted that another eminent southern historian, Clement Eaton, offers a contrary viewpoint in *Freedom of Thought in the Old South*). Calhoun, therefore, is controversial because the original political thinking he did during the first half of the nineteenth century was associated either with causes that were defeated or were thought to offend the essence of the American democratic faith. He deserves to be heard, however, not because he was correct on race relations (he was not), nor because he defended minority rights out of a love of liberty for all men (he did not); he deserves to be heard because he is virtually the only American statesman (other than perhaps Herbert Hoover) who saw what many Americans have only lately begun to see: that —as Alexis de Tocqueville warned—the worst tyranny to be feared in the American political system is the tyranny of the majority. This is an important matter, because it is the tyranny of the majority in the present state of Northern Ireland that Catholics protest; and similarly, Protestants in Northern Ireland fear unity with the Irish Republic precisely because they believe that they would be tyrannized by the Catholic majority.

Calhoun, it is interesting to observe, was born in 1782 in South Carolina into a Scots-Irish family whose members had emigrated from the north of Ireland in the middle of the eighteenth century. They had originally gone to Pennsylvania, but later moved to the southern "back country." After an education at Yale, he returned to practice law in South Carolina. He soon entered politics and was sent to Congress in 1810. During the next four decades he was a major force in American politics, serving as a congressman, senator, secretary of war, secretary of state, and Vice-President. At the beginning of his career he was an ardent supporter of federal authority and national unity. However, as the South became more and more dependent on the cotton economy (and therefore on slavery) Calhoun realized that the South was evolving into a region that was becoming very different from the rest of the United States. That divergence of his region, and the fear that that region would not be treated fairly by a national government controlled by the interests of other regions, caused the movement of Calhoun's political philosophy in the direction that would result in the Civil War.

It was the tariff, not cotton and slavery, that began the process in Calhoun's mind. The passage of the exorbitant "tariff of abominations" in 1828 was so discriminatory to the South that Calhoun joined the issue with his now famous *South Carolina Exposition and Protest*. In the 1850s, in the full flush of the debate over the institution of slavery, Calhoun wrote *Discourse on the Constitution and Government of the United States* and *A Disquisition on Government*. The three essays form a piece if one sees in them Calhoun's basic thrust: that some restraint on the unchecked control of government by the majority must be found in order to allow a minority some constitutional remedy for retaining freedom of action. Rather than one majority, Calhoun believed, there ought to be a "concurrent majority," a system that would prevent one or several interests from tyrannizing another. *In A Disquisition on Government*, he wrote:

> To do this each division or sector of the political organism should have either the right to a concurrent voice in legislative and policy formulation or, if not this, a decisive veto power over the majority. The different orders, classes or sectors of political society must end their conflict and struggles by concurring or agreeing as to aims before any meaningful action of the body politic can be undertaken.

The American political system, of course, was never required to give a constitutional answer to Calhoun's philosophy. Rather, the constitutional issue was settled militarily at Fort Sumter, Gettysburg, and Appomattox; it is possible that that was the only way in which it could have been settled. But no other way was ever seriously attempted, and once settled in that way, such ideas were forever regarded as illegitimate. While we may concede that Calhoun's defense of a minority section of the country was conceived in a circumstance and for a reason that has little positive relevance to our own time, the pamphlets written more than a century ago speak clearly to the contemporary world situation, which witnesses the desire of minorities to be freed from the tyranny of the majority (e.g., Nigeria, Pakistan, Viet Nam, South Africa, and Northern Ireland, to name only a few). But the difficulty in these cases, and in Calhoun's case, consists in defining a "state" or a "people," and then in knowing what consequences ought to follow once the definitions are agreed upon.

In the case of Northern Ireland, Senator Kennedy believes that the historic principle of self-determination is being abused by the British because the people of the six counties are not "a people" in "a state." The only "people" to which Kennedy will agree is a unified Irish people. Since Ulster is, in the Senator's view, "an uncouth entity," he will not hear of granting it self-determination; rather, he asks, "Why not self-determination for Londonderry, or County Tyrone, or any other Catholic area in Ulster?" Such a question is rather carping, because, as the Senator must realize, it can evoke the following response: "Why not self-determination for Belfast, or County Antrim, or any other Protestant area in Ulster?" The answers to the questions are not easy, and, as noted above, the resolution of them depends on how the interpreter will view presuppositional definitions of "people"

and "state," and how the rights of minorities can be safeguarded. One must concede to Senator Kennedy that the
Protestants of Northern Ireland are less convincing in
worrying about safeguarding their rights as a minority in
a future all-Ireland republic while they show little concern for the rights of the minority in Ulster (just as Calhoun's defense of the South's rights seems hollow when
one recalls the institution of slavery). By the same token,
however, it would seem ill-advised to force the Protestants
of Ulster into a minority status without due consideration
of minority rights (just as it did not really solve the constitutional problem in the United States to bludgeon the
South into a minority and an historically inferior position
vis-à-vis the other regions of the nation).

The simple truth, perhaps unpalatable to Irish nationalists, is that there has been and is an historic Protestant
presence in Ireland, which, because of its minority status,
views its identity in terms of unity with the other parts of
the United Kingdom. Senator Kennedy and others who
dream of Irish unity tell the Protestants of the North that
they *ought* to feel kinship with their Irish brothers to the
South; the plain fact is that they do not. In the impenetrable past the Protestants were implanted in Ireland, a
movement fraught with tragic consequences for Irish history; but it is now too late to ask them to "go back where
they came from." Senator Kennedy and his Irish constituency in America must surely be sensitive to this: there
were Protestants in Ireland long before the great migration brought the Catholic Irish to New England, but there
is no legitimacy to the suggestion that Irish-Americans go
back to Ireland. All Americans are faced with current
circumstances that are the result of an historic process of
the mingling of migratory peoples. Perhaps, because the
situation in Ireland is part of a larger story of human
tragedy, it may be impossible to resolve. But if the situation is to be brought to some acceptable conclusion, it will
be neither on the basis of the naked abuse of power by

Ulster Protestants, nor on the basis of the shouting of nationalistic and democratic slogans by Irish Catholics on both sides of the Atlantic.

Even less acceptable than Senator Kennedy's constitutional arguments, in our view, are his suggestions of American involvement in the resolution of the problems of Ulster. He writes:

> There are those who say that America should stand silent in the face of the daily tragedy taking place in Northern Ireland. I do not agree. . . . Our heritage as citizens in a nation that has been a spokesman for peace and human liberty in the world for two centuries requires us to speak out and find a helpful role to play in contributing to a permanent peace in Ulster. A larger issue is the question of what kind of foreign policy we want for America as we enter the final quarter of this century. I believe we want a policy that places far more emphasis on the billions of ordinary people throughout the world who seek a decent life. . . . In my view, it is time to let America's voice be heard. We should establish a continuing public tone in the foreign policy of the Administration, a tone that reflects the legitimate concerns of millions of American citizens for an end to the violence in Northern Ireland and a recognition that the minority in Ulster is entitled to participate fully in the government of their province. . . . In the long run we should leave no doubt of our support for unification as the ultimate goal for Ireland. . . . Until a political solution is implemented that is seen to be fair and even-handed by both sides, the search for peace will be in vain. Fifty-five thousand Americans died before we learned that tragic lesson in Vietnam, and four years of needless violence and destruction have passed while Britain learned that lesson in Northern Ireland.

In responding to Senator Kennedy we should repeat, as previously noted, that we share his notion that Americans of various backgrounds and persuasions have a right, perhaps even an obligation, to speak out on Northern Ireland, and that the problems there are not exclusively the "internal affairs" of the United Kingdom. However, we would nevertheless encourage the Senator and those likely to listen to him to be very wary of ideas which, however attractive, would tend to commit American public opinion and diplomacy to one side of the dispute in Ulster. We are concerned, because in doing so the Senator may run the risk of continuing some of the less helpful tendencies of twentieth-century American internationalism.

If it is true that our heritage in the United States has been as a spokesman for "human liberty in the world," it should be pointed out that the world has not asked us to be that spokesman; it is a burden we have imposed upon ourselves. It is a responsibility we assumed because it accorded well with our naive conception of ourselves and the superiority of our institutions. Thomas Jefferson foresaw a time when the young, vibrant, and pure institutions of the United States would have to send their spokesmen back to Europe whence our immigrant ancestors had come, in order to redeem the old, decrepit, and decadent institutions of Europe. That time came during World War I, at least in the view of President Wilson, who saw American participation as vital because the struggle was one to save humanity: thus, it was "the war to end all wars," "the war to make the world safe for democracy." In World War II, America's participation as "the arsenal of democracy" was required to defeat international fascism; but that was only a prelude to America's postwar role as self-appointed spokesman of opposition to international Communism. Both American political parties have subscribed to that role, and they have given a general American commitment to the world.

President John F. Kennedy gave the most articulate rendering of that commitment in his inaugural address: "We will go anywhere, pay any price, support any friend, oppose any foe. . . ." Those of us who cheered the young President in 1961 did not realize, as perhaps even he did not, that having said that, the first steps toward our agonizing involvement in Vietnam—at least in our imaginations—had already been taken. Because of his assassination, Kennedy was not forced to encounter the contradiction that faced those who remained and participated in the "agonizing reappraisal" by the end of the decade. Having confronted ourselves in the rice paddies of Vietnam, many of us discovered that there was another American tradition that did not view the United States as the self-appointed "spokesman for liberty" or the arbiter for the problems of the world. John Quincy Adams believed that America should not go abroad in search of dragons to slay, because she would thus no longer be mistress of her own spirit. Herbert Hoover believed that toleration of differences in the world accorded better with the American character than attempts to impose American solutions by either military diplomacy or dollar diplomacy.

President Kennedy, perhaps as he matured in office, also caught a glimpse of the vision in his beautiful speech at American University in 1963, which was a model of restraint and toleration. In that speech he did not dwell on the divisions caused by the cold war, but he looked forward to a world at peace—a peace that would not necessarily be universal accord but a process by which all parties agreed to solve problems.

> With such a peace, there will still be quarrels and conflicting interests, as there are within families and nations. World peace, like community peace, does not require that man love his neighbor—it requires only that they live together with mutual tolerance, submitting their disputes to a just and peaceful settlement.

It would be a peace that would not require the repeating of the slogans of the past, but rather a realistic understanding of the present: "We must deal with the world as it is, and not as it might have been had the history of the past . . . years been different."

Senator William Fulbright's essay on Vietnam (*The Arrogance of Power*) reminds us that there are two traditions, two heritages, regarding America's role in the world. One tradition would have the United States assume the responsibility that the "right" things be done in the world, whether or not the rest of the world shares our definition of what is right, or whether or not the United States *should* be the vehicle for the accomplishment of such "justice." The other tradition would have America assume its responsibilities in the world in a spirit of sympathy, understanding, and toleration—a position that is not mere isolationism. The internationalists would have us believe that any lowering of the dominant American profile in the world would be a retreat to isolationism and parochialism. That is certainly a danger to be avoided, but it can be avoided if American leaders realize that the United States, a nation with a substantial number of its own problems, does not own the patent to the solutions of the rest of mankind's problems.

To Senator Edward Kennedy one could reply that the larger issue is precisely "what kind of foreign policy we want for America as we enter the final quarter of this century." The Senator warns that if we retreat from internationalism "we deny our heritage"; but that is only one tradition in our heritage. It is conspicuously ironic that the Senator invokes the "lesson" of Vietnam as the reason we should involve ourselves in Northern Ireland. One would have thought that the "lesson" of Vietnam would surely have instructed us to be wary of a blustering intervention into the sensitive relationships of a partitioned nation. In thinking thus, however, one is invoking the other tradition of our heritage, a tradition of toleration and restraint that commends itself for our consideration. Of course, in stating this position we should not overemphasize the antithesis between the two traditions. There are several examples of their compatibility, such as the Marshall Plan and the Berlin Airlift. But in both of those instances the United States was helping people confront a real and relatively clearly defined danger. Problems come when an outside power enters a nation's internal strife with prefigured solutions that do not accord well with the historic situation that produced the conflict.

The near future in Northern Ireland may well prove to be a watershed in the province's history. After a period of direct rule from London and the creation of a short-lived "new assembly" with a power-sharing executive, elections are soon to take place for a constitutional convention. The burning question in Ulster today is whether or not the Protestants, mostly represented by the various factions of the Unionist party, can work together with the Catholics, largely represented by the Social Democratic and Labour party. This may be Ulster's last chance; for as Mr. Callaghan, the British Foreign Secretary, recently said in London, "Britain cannot bleed forever." *The London Times* noted in its sensitive and sensible editorial (June 21, 1973) that "there are no soft options in Ulster," but rather difficult and painful steps toward reconciliation that will require herculean efforts of compromise, graciousness, toleration, and good will from all parties in Britain, Northern Ireland, and the Republic of Ireland. As Messrs. Wilson, Faulkner, Fitt, and Cosgrave try to guide their respective constituencies through the difficult months ahead, they deserve our sympathy, understanding, and prayers. It would be tragic if American interference at this most sensitive time in any way impeded efforts by the people of Northern Ireland to be reconciled to each other.

While Senator Kennedy is correct in his assertion that the international migration of Irish peoples has internationalized the problem of Ulster, and while many Americans, whether or not they are of Irish or British ancestry, are very interested in the outcome, and while many may share the Senator's general belief that unity in an all-Ireland republic may be the island's last and best hope, we must nevertheless maintain that there are inherent difficulties in approaching this situation with prefigured solutions, especially when they come from the United States in the name of "human liberty." Since Protestantism and Catholicism have become the badges for the sectarian conflict in Northern Ireland, we believe that it is important for persons who are committed Christians to join the debate. This is not to say that because we are Christians we have the answers; on the contrary, we are painfully aware of how difficult the answers are to grasp. It is to say that as Christians we should help in any way we can in the work of the kingdom of God, which offers men the potential of being reconciled both to God and to each other.

It may be that the tragedy of Northern Ireland is today working inexorably toward some conclusion. The issues that divide the people there have been a burden to successive generations of British and Irish people on both sides of the Atlantic, as well as to sensitive human beings everywhere. We would hope that Senator Kennedy's understandable concern for justice in Ulster will not necessarily find him committed as a partisan in the historic cleavage there. Rather, we would hope that he might use his unique position to help, through quiet but resolute diplomacy, the reconciliation of the peoples on the Irish island in whatever constitutional and social arrangements may be best suited to promote the general welfare. We would hope that if he and the peoples of North America assume the burden of Northern Ireland, they do it in an understanding, sympathetic, even prayerful way.

3 LIFE IN NORTHERN IRELAND

> There are two communities in Northern Ireland,
> different in their origins, nursing different his-
> torical myths, possessing distinguishable cultures,
> having different songs and heroes, and wearing
> different denominations of the same religion. Re-
> ligion is the clearest badge of these differences.
> But the conflict is not *about* religion. It is about
> the self-assertion of two distinct communities, one
> of which is dominant in the public affairs of the
> province.
>
> —*The London Times*, August 30, 1969.

"*WHAT ARE THE PEOPLE* of Northern Ireland really
like?" Those who ask me this question often appear
slightly skeptical about my reply. For in the opinion of
most people the Irish, particularly those in the North, are
a hard-drinking, fairly unpleasant lot who will revert to
tribal religious customs at the drop of a crucifix. Nothing
could be further from the truth. They are generally decent,
hard-working, friendly people—good neighbors, whose
main characteristic is their kindness. Their tragedy is
that it is they on whom "the sins of their forefathers" are
being visited. However, they are also an insecure people,
and many of them do not really understand the intercon-

nections between the spiritual, moral, and social values they prize. Nor do they understand the viewpoints of those who hold different values. Consequently, they have become insular and at times defensively aggressive, lest their inadequacy become exposed for all to see. In these ways they are really no different from people in the rest of Britain or, for that matter, anywhere else in the world.

The purpose of this chapter will be to consider the views, prejudices, and practices of average Ulstermen—both Protestant and Catholic. We will use these labels to identify them, bearing in mind, as the quotation from *The Times* indicates, that the conflict is not simply about religion, and bearing in mind also that there are broad spectra of opinions within both communities. We should realize, however, that any other labels would be equally misleading generalities. Through these "average" men the political, religious, social, economic, and psychological attitudes and behavior of Ulster's two communities may be described.

Some may argue that no such "average" person exists. Certainly the events of the last five years have considerably changed people's outlooks, and today's average man is a very different person from the one of ten years ago. Secondly, many people born and raised in Northern Ireland may well point out that this or that "average" characteristic is not true of them. Nevertheless, it is often necessary to speak in general terms, provided, of course, they are as accurate as possible, in order that those who are not directly concerned in a given situation, and sometimes even those who are, can more readily understand the issues involved. And we feel that understanding of Northern Ireland and its problems is a paramount need today. It can provide the only basis for the dialogue and accommodation that are presently missing both in Ulster and Britain, and in Eire's dealings with Ulster.

POLITICS

All the people of Northern Ireland are British. They owe allegiance to Queen Elizabeth II, are represented at Westminster, and pay their taxes just as do the people who live in Cardiff, Edinburgh, or London. This is a constitutional and political fact of life. Yet only the Protestants feel British—and this is another political fact of life. A survey, published in 1971 in Professor Richard Rose's book *Governing Without Consensus*, showed that about 70% of all Protestants approved of Northern Ireland's constitution; the figure for Catholics was about 30%.

Historically, as we have seen, the province comprises two distinct groups of people: descendants of the native Catholic Irish and descendants of the transplanted Protestant English and Scots. In Ulster today these divisions continue to be clearly apparent. The 1961 census showed that there were in Northern Ireland 413,000 Presbyterians, 345,000 Church of Ireland members, and 72,000 Methodists, as well as 498,000 Roman Catholics. The latter still resent the "invasion" that cost them their land; the others still despise the traditions and religion of the natives. Thus, the primary cause of tension was, and in a sense still is, ethnic. Unfortunately, this is not a situation unique to Ulster, as citizens of Spain, South Africa, Rhodesia, the United States, Russia, England, Australia, and India—to mention but a few—can testify. In Northern Ireland it just happens that the easiest peg on which to hang these differences is religion rather than the more usual pegs of skin color or regional loyalty. This centuries-old ethnic division colors all contemporary thinking. One faction equates England's ruling of Ireland with colonialism, chauvinism, and economic subjection; the other sees it as an exercise in loyalty and in preserving national boundaries, coupled with an attempt to civilize the "natives."

History, therefore, plays a perhaps unduly large part in

Irish politics, Yet the lessons it teaches are themselves often obscured by sectarian thinking. In some cases people are given different interpretations of the same event. To unionists, Connolly's socialism was simply a development of the anarchy of the French Revolution. To republicans it was the only sensible reaction to the exploitation of absentee English landlords. In other cases people, especially children, are taught only those aspects of history that are considered "beneficial," and events are seldom set in their full context. Thus, one group of children learns about Cromwell's massacres at Drogheda and Wexford, the callousness of the British government during the great famine, and the "thuggery" of the Black and Tans. The other group is nurtured on the glorious Protestant victory at the Boyne, the sacrifice of hundreds of loyal Ulstermen at the Battle of the Somme in 1916, and the treason of the Easter Rebellion in the same year.

It is hardly surprising that in such a blinkered society the dominant political issues are most frequently thought of in terms of security. Catholics in the North feel insecure because they are a minority; as a result they turn for help and moral support to their kinfolk in the South. And this action is immediately interpreted by unionists as an act of betrayal. Unionists feel insecure also, and for the same reason. They constitute a minority within the whole of Ireland and so look to Britain for support. This, in turn, is viewed by the Irish as the natural action of a colonial and puppet state. Thus, the cycle is completed and revolves remorselessly towards destruction.

But why should this be? Let us first consider the Protestant viewpoint. The Unionist party has governed Northern Ireland since its inception, and the ratio of Unionist members of parliament to nationalists, of whatever party, has always been greater than the ratio of Protestants to Catholics in the province. Such a situation caused no surprise in the first decade or two following partition. After all, Ulster was primarily established as a Protestant country for Protestants. (Monaghan, Donegal, and Cavan were excluded from the historic Ulster when the present Northern Ireland boundaries were drawn up, because the 1911 census indicated that the people in these counties were 74.7%, 78.9%, and 81.5% Catholic respectively. The number of Catholics these figures represented would have dangerously lowered the size of the Protestants' overall majority in the province.) Also, the early refusal of many Catholics to acknowledge the state's authority helped to reduce their representation. The continuing under-representation of Catholic interests, however, is due in large part to their disillusionment with the way the state has evolved, to the refusal of many to vote (Protestant view), and to political gerrymandering (Catholic view).

The reason for unionist dominance has been quite simply "the border." The Unionist party, as its name implies, stands for union with Britain. Over the years, the party has skillfully pre-empted the political middle ground. It has also so presented political issues that every decision has carried with it constitutional implications. That is to say, support for the Unionist position has been coupled with the imperative of continued links with Britain. Support for any other position, no matter how plausible, has been projected as undermining the authority of the Unionist party—and thus the union—which alone could be trusted to preserve and defend the loyalists. Thus, for example, the Northern Ireland Labour party has languished because it has been unable successfully to separate industrial relations from the larger issue of the state's existence in the minds of most people.

Unionists have decried the notion that the Labour party can just seek to raise the lot of the working man, irrespective of his religion. Each Protestant vote for Labour splits the loyalist front, so the slogan goes, and may allow Catholics to assume power. Until the recent assembly elections, Ulster Protestants never dissented from this political theory. Consequently, every election has been fought ultimately not on social and economic issues but on the constitutional one. Faced with the choice of preserving or dismantling the state, or believing that they were faced with such a choice, Protestants voted the Unionist position. Safety could only be found in solidarity.

The *Belfast News-Letter* can claim with considerable justification to have faithfully reflected majority Protestant opinion through the years. The following excerpts from its editorial pages set the mood and illustrate this single issue theme on which elections have been fought.

- The issue at stake in this election must be apparent to all. Do the Ulster people still value their birthright? Are they still insistent on retaining their full partnership with the rest of the United Kingdom within the Empire? In neither case is the issue in doubt. There remains the question which tomorrow must settle: Is the Government that for twelve years has stood, and continues to stand, for the conservation of that birthright to receive a mandate not less emphatic than before. . . . The electorate must not be deceived by those who are not Unionist Party members or supporters. . . . Every such vote (for them) is a symptom of weakness and indecision and will be regarded as such by (Ulster's) enemies. (1933)
- From whatever angle the general election in Northern Ireland be regarded, the Constitutional question emerges as the governing issue. (1945)
- Today Ulster people go to the poll on an issue which admits of no compromise—whether they are to continue in Union with Great Britain or to be absorbed into an Irish Republic. Never throughout the long controversy has their position been challenged more directly; at no time has the need for an unequivocal reply been more urgent. (1949)

- Not the least disturbing feature of the present General Election campaign has been an increasing tendency to suggest that as Northern Ireland's position is now unassailable, the time has come when the Unionist electorate can dismiss its fears and with safety concentrate upon purely domestic issues. No more pernicious theory could be advanced; no policy is more fraught with danger. (1953)
- While the leader of the Northern Ireland Labour Party has declared that one of its objects is to preserve and strengthen the Province's link with Great Britain, the fact remains that it is challenging candidates whose attitude towards the maintenance of the Border cannot be called into question, and has abstained from opposing men who would like to see Ulster absorbed by an all-Ireland Republic. (1958)

The extent to which union with Britain and loyalty to the crown have been made the preserve of the Unionist party was indicated by a 1966 survey. It showed that 82% of all Protestants voted, and 81% voted Unionist. Only 2% of Catholics voted Unionist, and 40% did not vote at all. Over the years unionism also became symbolically and actually linked with both the Orange Order and the existence of a separate government at Stormont. The Orange Order is deeply involved in the religious and political life of the community. Each Orange lodge has a chaplain, and its membership is frequently drawn from local church congregations, though there is no official link between the lodge and the church. Nevertheless, the lodges' strong religious emphasis is highly significant, not least in the eyes of Catholics. For the Orange Order is committed to the Protestant ascendancy, and phrases like "no surrender" and "not an inch" fall easily from the lips of its members. In fact, before joining a lodge a man must agree to "love, uphold and defend the Protestant religion . . . [and] strenuously oppose the fatal errors and doctrines of the Church of Rome. . . ."

The order's political influence is likewise considerable, because membership in it is virtually a requirement for Unionist M.P.'s and those aspiring to join their ranks. Perhaps it is only by insisting on this precondition that many rank and file Protestants feel assured that their government will not step outside the primary objective of Orangeism: "to maintain the laws and peace of the country and the Protestant constitution." Even those Protestants who feel that the order is a divisive and negative force would be quick to acknowledge its powerfulness. Stormont's importance, on the other hand, was both practical and symbolic. Before its abolition it consisted of a fifty-two seat house of commons and a twenty-six seat senate, which had the power to pass laws for "the peace, order and good government of Northern Ireland" (Government of Ireland Act, 1920), subject to certain limitations. However, it was not only the laws it passed but also the fact that it could pass them that was important to most unionists.

The glistening white building in its immaculately kept grounds, in which Ulstermen regulated their lives without fear of political subjection, symbolized their independence from both Dublin and London. In the case of the former, Stormont's very presence soothed their fears by reminding and reassuring them of the continuing reality of "the border." As far as London was concerned, Stormont was a bulwark: while it functioned, any attempt by Britain to try to reunite Ireland could easily be thwarted. It was the existence of these sentiments that provoked the outcry from Ulster's loyalists when Stormont was suspended. All their anxieties about betrayal again flooded to the surface. And subsequent statements by British ministers and ex-ministers concerning the eventual reunification of Ireland, an all-Ireland council, and even integration with Britain have positively accentuated the apprehensive and skeptical feelings Ulstermen have toward British intentions.

Finally, it should be understood that the commitment of Ulster's Protestants to their political heritage has not been diminished by the present troubles. They are in no mood to seek peace at any price. Even the most "ordinary" citizens regularly combine expressions of dismay and despair over their present plight with a steely determination not to give in to the IRA. This determination was made clear by the large majority that voted in the 1973 plebiscite to retain the province's ties with Great Britain. Its strength, however, was more clearly revealed by Professor Rose's survey. He found that 52% of Protestants endorsed the use of any methods, including violence, to keep Northern Ireland Protestant. And 73% of the members of the Orange Order were in this category.

The other major factor reinforcing the Protestants' commitment is the belief that their position has been grossly misrepresented by much of the world's press. Repeatedly, they argue, newsmen have resorted to sloganeering, the use of emotive catch words—"civil rights" and "ghetto" are two that are particularly offensive—and oversimplifications. Protestants feel they have been invariably classified as "baddies" and Catholics, even at the height of the IRA campaigns, as "oppressed goodies." Such allegedly biased reporting has caused Protestants to close ranks, to feel that no one is concerned with discovering the truth or appreciating their legitimate viewpoint. Despite their contribution to Ulster's troubles, stretching back over fifty years, the Protestants argue that they have been more "sinned against than sinning." They believe that they should not be made scapegoats for the conflict, to which they are only one party. Neither the press, nor even British governments, should feel that easy solutions can be found by pressuring the Protestants to become the kind of people whom those not involved in the past or present of Northern Ireland would find more congenial.

Constitutionally, as we have said, the Catholics and nationalists who live in Ulster are also British. They too vote in Westminster parliamentary elections and had a say with Protestants in who was elected to Stormont and, more recently, to the new assembly. But they "feel" Irish. To them the border that divides "their" country is an artificial barrier that was imposed by Britain as an expedient reaction to Protestant blackmail. They want it abolished. Politically, the Catholic working man wants nothing to do with the Unionist party, because he believes it speaks against his interests. He wants political unity with the South for a whole series of reasons that can best be summed up in the word "Ireland." For to him Ireland is more than a geographical entity. It has a spiritual and cultural identity of which he feels a part; early made aware of this heritage, he wants fully to enter into it.

What Catholics see as the sham democracy of the North alienates them and strengthens their desire to be free. They know that they will be effectively excluded from governing in the foreseeable future. (This is being written at a time when "power-sharing" remains an unproved political concept.) Since the province votes along strictly sectarian lines (the Alliance party notwithstanding), and since Protestants outnumber Catholics by a ratio of roughly two to one, Catholics cannot hope to achieve political power. This political impotence has driven many to seek influence through organizations such as the CRA and the IRA. Even the occasional electoral victories of Sinn Fein candidates, who then refused to take their seats, only added to Catholic frustration by underscoring the essential futility of the republicans' position.

To Catholics, the first two demands of the CRA in 1968 really expressed the nub of their political problem. These demands were for the introduction of a universal franchise in local government elections and the redrawing of local election boundaries. They were made because, unlike the voting systems used in the two parliamentary elections, universal suffrage did not then apply in local elections. This fact formed the basis for the highly effective, but in view of the circumstances somewhat misleading, rallying cry "one man, one vote," which helped to endear the Catholics' cause to people throughout the world. In order to vote at the local level, an elector had to qualify as the owner or tenant of a dwelling house, land, or premises subject to certain conditions. This qualification had the effect of reducing those eligible to vote from about 900,000 to about 700,000. Now there is nothing in these restrictions of a political nature per se. The economic limitations were designed to express the sociological concept that only those with a direct interest in a community should be allowed a say in how that community is run. However, if we remember that Northern Ireland was established as a "Protestant" country, and that, generally, more of the wealth belongs to Protestants, we can see that the effect of economic restrictions on voting will not be uniformly distributed throughout the community. Catholics will theoretically be disenfranchised more heavily, and this in fact was the case. Further, since local authorities control such things as housing, education, and social services, the disadvantage experienced by Catholics under these Protestant-controlled authorities could be severe. Thus, in a real sense Catholics felt themselves cut off from and unable to attain political power.

This feeling was increased by the alleged practice that prompted the second CRA demand. Many Catholics believe and claim that Unionists used their local council control to gerrymander local election boundaries. Carefully drawn ward boundaries could ensure Protestant control of a council even if the majority of the citizens in its area were Catholic. Barritt and Carter, in their excellent book *The Northern Ireland Problem* (1962), question the validity of these claims. By 1969, however, the *Report of the Cameron Commission on Disturbances in Northern Ireland* indicated that, in their view, a minority of councils were guilty of this practice. They made the following comment on one example of manipulation of electoral boundaries:

> The most glaring case was Londonderry County Borough where sixty per cent of the adult population was Catholic but where sixty per cent of the seats on the Corporation were held by Unionists. These results were achieved by the use, for example, of ward areas in which Unionist representatives were returned by small majorities, whereas non-Unionist representatives were returned by very large majorities.

In Londonderry County Borough in 1967, 14,429 Catholic voters and 8,781 other voters returned twelve Unionists and eight non-Unionists! Even though local election voting restrictions have now been removed and local election boundaries have been reviewed by the Macrory Committee, Catholics' feeling that they have suffered political discrimination has in no way decreased their aspirations for a united Ireland.

During the province's existence, the major political pressure in behalf of Catholics has been exerted by the Dublin government. It has never recognized the legitimacy of a separate Ulster and has continually championed the cause of its detached brethren. The government's refusal to act decisively against the IRA in its sporadic attempts to "liberate" the North, and its intransigence over the question of extradition have left no doubt where its sympathies lie. Catholic political leadership in the North may even have suffered because of the tendency of the people to look to Dublin for guidance. With the emergence of the

Social Democratic and Labour party, however, that leadership is firmly back in local hands. This, generally speaking, was the position in 1969. Protestants voted together—for Unionists—to ensure separation from the Republic and the maintenance of ties with Great Britain, while the Orange Order guarded the purity of the political faith. Catholics, if they chose or were able to vote, voted for an assortment of nationalist and republican parties whose common goal was to reunite Ireland and finally rid it of British imperialism.

Since 1969, political feeling has become further polarized. Protestants, outraged by the campaign of killing and terror, have become increasingly "right-wing." The solidarity of the Unionist party cracked in 1969 when official and unofficial Unionists stood against each other. From that split two groups have emerged. One, under the leadership of Brian Faulkner, seeks to continue traditional Unionist policies—once thought extreme by many, but in today's political climate offered as almost moderate. The other, led by Ian Paisley, William Craig, and an ever changing number of militant workers, not to mention Enoch Powell, is more adamantly loyalist and given to speculation about the possibilities of a unilateral declaration of independence on the one hand and total integration with Britain on the other.

Catholics, terrified by the brutality of the early Protestant attacks, initially welcomed the British Army as saviors. Not long afterwards, however, they turned to the IRA for protection and made both physical and political secession and the gun their political weapons. Eventually, under the tutelage of Gerry Fitt, John Hume, Austin Currie, and others, they were persuaded to transfer their allegiance to the SDLP. This allowed the SDLP to obtain about 30% representation in the since disbanded new assembly. By voting in such large numbers, Catholics firmly rejected an IRA call to boycott the elections. It would be dangerous to assume, though, that the IRA no longer enjoys considerable support.

Thus, politically speaking, Ulster is bitterly divided today and will remain so for some considerable time. The ability of the proposed constitutional convention to provide a viable forum for decision-making and power-sharing, the Whitelaw-Rees answer to Protestant power concentration, is still to be determined. On its degree of success may depend the very political future of Northern Ireland.

RELIGION

There are approximately two Protestants to one Catholic in Northern Ireland, and just about everyone claims to be religious. In the 1951 census, only sixty-four people out of 1,370,921 claimed to be atheists. In 1971, 86% of Ulster people believed that God watches over what each person does and thinks, compared to 49% with this belief in the rest of Britain. A 1959 survey of Queens University students, who are perhaps as representatively religious as any other group, showed that 94% of Catholics and 50-55% of Protestants attended church. It would seem accurate to conclude that, if these figures are even reasonably representative of the community, the percentage of Ulster churchgoers is very much higher than that in England. This may make it difficult for the English to understand why religion is so important to the Irish. And this importance becomes even greater when one takes account of religion's historical role in shaping Irish society.

People within both religious communities can be divided into two categories. There are those to whom the faith is real and vital: they have a personal knowledge of God that gives significance and purpose to life. Secondly, there are those to whom religion is little more than a social ritual and who seek only to identify with a particular church "brand name." The latter know little of what they are supposed to believe but are quick to recite the "errors" of the other man's creed. It is primarily they, rather than the former, who make religion the inflammatory point in the society. The Christians for their part are content, with some notable exceptions, to discuss and disagree on theology and church government.

Let us then first consider the views of the majority. The average Protestant, if he has any theological knowledge or understanding, sees himself and his beliefs in the tradition of the Reformation. In his opinion, Martin Luther was one of the most significant figures of ecclesiastical history. And he feels that in Luther's stand against Roman Catholicism his own freedom of worship was procured. That freedom having been established, he holds that certain doctrines naturally follow from it. These include the sole and sufficient authority of the Bible in all matters of faith and conduct, the right of an individual Christian to approach God directly, and the assurance that Christian believers—those who have a personal trust in Jesus Christ—can know God's forgiveness for their sins. Finally, the average Protestant rejects as unbiblical the role of tradition in the Roman Catholic Church, the idea of papal infallibility, the "theory" of the transubstantiation of the sacraments, and the right of the church to control private morals. All these doctrines, of course, are bound together theologically, though the vast majority of Protestants are not able to explain why this should be so. Nevertheless, they passionately believe them to be true. With the zeal of new converts (despite the centuries since Luther), they spurn, often with open hostility, the religious system from which they have been "freed." Rightly or wrongly, they see in the Roman Church an exclusivity and authoritarianism that fundamentally contradicts the tenets of their faith. As far as the church's relationship to the state is concerned, Protestants resent the Catholic position as outlined by the Most Rev. Dr. Sheehan in his *Apologetics and Christian Doctrine:*

> The Church, commissioned by Christ to preach the Gospel, and clothed with infallibility, can never be unwilling to suppress erroneous doctrine. The Church and every lover of truth must necessarily be intolerant of error.

This Catholic intolerance toward "error" was given more practical substance by Jesuit Father Cavalli in *La Civilta Catholica* in 1948. He wrote:

> In a State where the majority of the people are Catholic, the Church asks that error shall not be accorded a legal existence, and that if religious minorities exist they shall be accorded a *de facto* existence only, not the opportunity of spreading their beliefs.

Thus, the lines of religious dispute are clearly drawn, and their connection with Irish politics is quite obvious. In a united Ireland, Protestants would be in a minority and therefore vulnerable to Catholic pressure. Furthermore, because the Catholic Church is recognized in the South as the "State Church" (it was until recently accorded a special place in the republic's constitution), and because its influence and precepts still play a large part in molding Eire's public policy, Northern Protestants naturally feel that their most cherished beliefs would be undermined in any all-Ireland union.

The average Catholic sees his religious faith validated by two thousand years of history and tradition. He traces his church establishment back to the direct command to Peter from Jesus himself that the apostle should be the rock on which the Christian church should be built (an interpretation hotly disputed by Protestants). As a consequence, he sees no inconsistency in allowing those who have followed Peter's example and have been directly instructed by God to educate and teach him what God expects of him. Nor does he have any reason to think that the Pope, whom he believes to be Peter's direct successor, should be in any doubt as to what is the mind of God. On the contrary, Catholics find the social and religious services of their church both helpful and reassuring. And above all, they believe its teaching, so obviously linked to the Bible and the church's tradition, to be true. It is hardly surprising, therefore, that they should view Protestants— who, after all, deserted the church, not vice versa—as being in error. The fragmentation of Protestantism is just what they would expect to result from the holding of such heretical views.

In his book, Dr. Sheehan gives a balanced statement of the Catholic viewpoint.

> No man . . . who, on coming to know the true Church, refuses to join it can be saved. Neither can he be saved if, having once entered the Church, he forsakes it through heresy or schism. . . . He who severs himself from the Church severs himself from Christ, and cannot be saved, for in Christ alone is salvation. . . . [God, however,] will not condemn those who through inculpable ignorance are unaware of His precept, who serve Him faithfully according to their conscience, who have a sincere desire to do His will, and therefore, implicitly, the desire to become members of His Church. . . . [However,] in view of the fact that the Church stands plainly before the eyes of men like a city on a mountain top, that the words of her ministers have gone forth to the ends of the earth, we do not venture to say that such cases are typical of large numbers. We are certain, at all events, that for men deprived of the abundant graces at the disposal of those who belong to the visible membership of the Church, salvation is not easy.

From our brief survey we can see that the theological differences between Protestants and Catholics center on the view each holds of the Bible. All Protestants affirm the uniqueness and all-sufficiency of Scripture. The Catholic Church, in contrast, places itself alongside the Bible as the means of conveying God's revelation to men. This doctrinal variance, so unimportant to nonreligious people, remains the primary unresolved issue of Christendom. And from it these two presently irreconcilable traditions flow.

There are three major areas in which the theological differences already described are translated into emotionally charged social issues. These are education, interfaith marriage, and general morality. We shall consider each of them in turn.

Catholic and Protestant children are educated quite separately in Northern Ireland. A survey in 1960 showed that 41% of the school population was Catholic and 59% Protestant (this compared with 35% and 65% of the population respectively). Ninety-eight percent of all Catholic primary school children attended Catholic schools. After the eleven-plus examination, the religions were still kept apart in different secondary and grammar schools.

Ulster's segregated education is entirely due to the insistence of the Roman Catholic Church. It does not reflect any unwillingness on the part of the Northern Ireland government to discharge its responsibilities to one section of the community. In fact, the Government of Ireland Act prohibits the endowment of any religion and any preference or privilege, disability or disadvantage, to anyone on account of religious belief. From what has been said we can see that it would be impossible to teach in secular schools a religion that would be acceptable to everyone. The Catholic Church has made its position clear in the Catholic Canon Law, which includes the following statements:

- Parents have a most serious duty to secure a fully Catholic education for their children. . . .
- Catholic pupils are not to frequent non-Catholic schools or neutral schools or schools that are open also to non-Catholics. Only the Ordinary of the place where the school is situated is competent to determine, according to the instructions of the Apostolic See, in what circumstances it may be tolerated for Catholics to attend such schools and what safeguards are to be prescribed against the danger of perversion. . . .

Irish history contains numerous examples of devout men who believed, rightly or wrongly, that their religious principles were in conflict with their civic responsibilities and chose "to obey God rather than men." One of the more recent is the loyalist Protestant leader Rev. Ian Paisley, shown here leaving prison after serving a short term for refusing to pay a fine for unlawful assembly in Armagh in January 1969. While in prison, Rev. Paisley wrote his commentary on the Epistle to the Romans.

Thus, the church's requirement that Catholics be educated in Catholic schools is uncompromising. And because of the dominant influence of the Irish Catholic Church over its people, its wishes have substantially been carried out. Interestingly, evidence is now available, perhaps for the first time, that this segregated education is widely unpopular. Professor Rose found that 65% of all respondents in his survey were in favor of educating Protestant and Catholic children together, although five-sixths of them had themselves been educated in segregated schools. Among Catholics, 69% approved of integrated education—in flat contradiction to the views of the Catholic hierarchy.

Quite understandably, segregated education is viewed differently in the two communities. Catholics see it (or saw it) as a natural extension of what they believe. To them education involves more than merely learning the three R's; it includes training the will and developing spiritual and moral values. They consider it vital that children appreciate the complementary nature of what they learn and what they believe. In fact, many Catholics would go further and say that they want their children to have a Christian education, as opposed to the amoral, secular education offered by the state. (Their reasoning is almost identical to the reasoning of evangelicals in the United States who send their children to Christian schools and colleges.)

Protestants also believe in the unity of God's revelation and the need to develop spiritual understanding, but they emphasize the role the church and family should play in teaching that to their children. They view the desire for Catholic education as nothing more than a means of indoctrinating the children to accept socio-religious theories and historical interpretations that will eventually bias them against the state. They also see it as one more example of the Catholics' refusal to become integrated into the state's systems and further evidence of their anti-social behavior.

Whatever the reason for Catholics' compliance with their church's views, three consequences of immense social importance flow from separate education. First, it is perfectly understandable that Catholics should want to live near the schools their children attend. In fact, many cannot afford to live far from them. Nevertheless, this proximity increases the likelihood that the two communities will live in isolated enclaves apart from each other, and this situation naturally fosters sectarian feeling. Secondly, children, during the most impressionable and formative years of their lives, have no opportunity to meet those whose backgrounds are different from their own. There is no way for them to learn that the others are human beings of equal sensitivity and with equally genuine aspirations. Thus, the myths and prejudices of unenlightened and fearful people are perpetuated from generation to generation. And although students of strong and no religious conviction go to Ulster's two universities, by then it is often too late for any radical change to occur in the thinking of even this minority of the people. The third consequence of separate education is that it provides a means for those so inclined to covertly discriminate in employment. Let us offer an illustration of what form this may take. If a graduate of one of Belfast's grammar schools applies for a job in Northern Ireland, the first thing his prospective employer will request is his academic record —a perfectly legitimate request. Yet the very name of the applicant's school declares his religious position with a high degree of accuracy, and this information can then be used as a basis for discrimination. How bright the prospects for peaceful coexistence in Ulster can be while children are educated separately is a matter of considerable doubt.

The second controversial issue that stems from Protestant-Catholic theological differences is that of interfaith marriages. Such marriages could provide one means of truly integrating the two communities; yet few take place. The Catholics' attitude toward them, following naturally from what they believe, was set forth as long ago as 1564 in the Council of Trent. Since 1908, the Catholic Church has required that such marriages be solemnized in one of their churches and that both parties signify their agreement to the following points:

(i) There shall be no interference with the religion of the Catholic party or his (or her) practise of it.

(ii) The Catholic party shall endeavour in every reasonable way to bring the non-Catholic partner to the faith.

(iii) All the children of the marriage shall be baptized and brought up in the Catholic faith.

(iv) The parties shall not present themselves either before or after the Catholic marriage before a non-Catholic minister of religion for any religious ceremony.

[There were some minor modifications resulting from Vatican II.]

The requirement of Catholic education is generally included under the third of these points. Such a declaration is understandably resented strongly by Protestants. To them its rigidity and arrogance, as well as its theology, deny the whole basis of marriage, which is mutual sharing and responsibility. They also point out that, as in education and morality, it is not they but the Catholic Church that, by its rules and regulations, destroys the concept of normal community relations. Such few interfaith marriages as occur are consequently subject to all the pressures of a society that recognizes no compromise position. And these pressures are universally understood. A survey of Queens University students some years ago showed that, although seventy-eight percent claimed to have friends of the opposite faith, ninety-six percent were against intermarriage between members of the two communities.

The third socially divisive issue arising from the theological divide involves the different standards that govern the private, "moral" lives of the people. With varying degrees of enthusiasm, most Protestants accept such procedures as divorce and artificially induced contraception as an often necessary and unavoidable part of their humanity, and they regulate their lives accordingly. However, not only does the Catholic Church not support such policies; it actively seeks to prevent the Irish government from adopting them. The most famous example of this type of ecclesiastical pressure involved legislation that the then minister of health in Dublin, Dr. Noel Browne, proposed to introduce in 1950. His Mother and Child Bill included free maternity care and education in childbearing, aspects of which offended the church. Dr. Browne, believing that there was nothing in the bill that contravened the church's teaching, refused to withdraw it, and he was subsequently forced to resign. This involvement of the church in the private lives of its members as an extension of its pastoral concern is a completely acceptable activity to many Catholics, though their numbers may be decreasing. On the other hand, such direct moral persuasion is alien to the Protestant tradition. Hence, fear of Catholic-inspired, government-enforced morality is to Protestants another good reason for resisting the establishment of a united Ireland. Likewise, the fact that the political power of the Catholic Church is so great that it could cause the Dublin government to retreat is a specter that haunts most Protestants.

Finally, these different moral standards give rise to real community tensions. Catholic families are often very large and as a result are entitled to a higher proportion of state subsidies than their actual numbers might suggest. This is a continual source of irritation to Protestants, who mutter darkly about Catholics "sponging off the state" and fear that they will eventually be outnumbered in the province simply by being outbred.

Religious differences are thus central to the whole "problem" of Ireland. Yet they are not the only issue, despite what the media would have us believe. Neither are they as insignificant as many conservative Christians would have us think. Religion, along with politics and economics, is a practical factor that divides the population and keeps it divided. Nevertheless, there are many Christians on both sides of that divide, and in this fact lies both the hope for and the tragedy of Ulster. (We will deal with the hope in the next section.) The tragedy is that these Christians generally do not recognize each other's existence. (We say "generally" because recently clergy have begun to get together informally, and Christians in both communities have had common charismatic experiences and prayer services.) That is to say, they have allowed doctrinal differences to assume greater significance in their thinking than the love of God and the unity of the Spirit, which bind both together in the true body of Christ. As a result, Christians have done little to moderate religious intolerance. To the extent that their attitudes reflect the inability of each one of us to show God's love to those with whom we disagree, we all stand condemned.

ECONOMICS AND SOCIAL HABITS

The two communities in Northern Ireland are inclined to live quite separately, especially in the towns. Perhaps it is worth pointing out, however, that this separatism, though undesirable, is not necessarily sinister. People naturally tend to live near those institutions that occupy a major

place in their lives—churches, schools, and places of
work. In addition, all of us choose as friends and neighbors people with whom we have things in common. A
Catholic Bogside or Protestant Sandy Row is no less pref-
erable in principle than a Jewish Golders Green in London
or an Irish district of New York or Boston. They all reflect
the human tendency to seek congenial surroundings. And
the reasons governing this desire need be no more insidious than those which cause towns to have a rich section or
a wrong side of the tracks. This inclination of people to
live "with their own kind" means that the two communities also socialize separately. There are sectarian pubs
and clubs that by choice as well as location cater almost
exclusively to either loyalists or republicans. In both
cases the appropriate cultural heritage and the version of
Irish history acceptable to the patrons are extolled, often
in songs whose words are at best highly offensive to the
other side. Fortunately for community relations, like at-
tracts like and complete mayhem is thus averted.

The social differences between the two groups are numerous. One of the most obvious is the divergence of their
attitudes toward Sunday. Ulster Protestants are fairly
puritanical in their outlook. They dress in their best
clothes to go to church, and they generally do little else
for the rest of the day. Many would not even work in
their gardens on a Sunday. This practice stems from
their belief in the ethic of rest on the Sabbath, combined
with a strong temperance background. It was brought
into sharp focus a few years ago by a furor in Belfast
over whether or not children's swings in public parks
should continue to be chained up from Saturday
evening until Monday morning, as was the custom. Catholics, on the other hand, have a much more flexible approach. They are quite prepared to use Sundays for rec-
reation, provided they have first attended mass. As a result, their sports events, entertainments, and local dances

are commonly held in certain parts of Belfast, while the rest of the city is completely closed.

Province-wide, music and arts societies and professional (though usually not amateur) theater groups are mixed, as are such sports as soccer. And boxers are loudly cheered or booed regardless of their places of worship. Rugby and cricket tend to be games that Protestants play; Gaelic football and hurling are decidedly Catholic.

Northern Ireland's economic progress over the past twenty years has been impressive. The government has attracted many new industries to the province by offering financial incentives. This successful policy has ensured a steady increase in manufacturing output. However, the problem of persistently heavy unemployment has so far defied solution. Consequently, although the annual rate of growth during 1950-62 was greater than in the rest of the United Kingdom, and real income per capita rose by about one-third, it was still 25% below the national average. Within the community, Protestants are better off than Catholics. (It should be remembered, though, that such a statement is based on average earnings and total unemployment figures. There are also many poor Protestants, but there are fewer middle and high income Catholics than Protestants.) Yet such a situation is not in itself evidence of financial malpractice. The bulk of Northern Ireland's wealth, both industrial and personal, has always been Protestant owned. Similarly, a majority of the province's leaders in all the major aspects of its life are Protestants. Thus, there has been an uneven division of the economic cake from Ulster's inception. That it should still be so merely reflects how inadequate normal economic forces are to produce economic equality, especially if contrary forces are also at work.

The following figures, quoted as examples of this economic disparity, are all drawn from Barritt and Carter's book *The Northern Ireland Problem*. The authors surveyed 2,481 people in Portadown in 1960 and classified them according to the five social class divisions (for employment) used by the registrar-general for England and Wales. Thirteen percent of all Catholics appeared in the top two categories, 55% in the bottom two. Comparable divisions for Protestants were Presbyterians 24% and 26%, Church of Ireland members 24% and 33%, and Methodists 21% and 21%. In 1959, of 740 people who held grades from staff officers up to permanent secretaries in the Northern Ireland Civil Service, 694 or 94% were Protestants. And in the same year a survey of the province's trade unions indicated that 20% of branch secretaries were Catholics and 80% Protestants. However, in the Amalgamated Transport and General Workers Union, with its large unskilled membership, 46% of branch secretaries were Catholics. Comparable figures for the Amalgamated Engineering Union and the Association of Supervisory Staffs, Executives, and Technicians were 12% and 9% respectively. While all these figures may have changed somewhat in the intervening years, the overall balance of wealth has not.

To offset the impression that the Catholics' economic difficulties are all of Protestant making, we should remember the other factors that are involved. Catholic families are generally much larger than Protestant ones, and therefore a given wage buys less per capita. Secondly, any disparity that exists between Catholic schools and state schools tends to favor the state system. Children going through the latter, mainly Protestants, are better equipped to compete for top jobs in the economic marketplace. Thirdly, a higher proportion of Catholics are unemployed because a higher percentage of them are unskilled or semiskilled. Towns such as Londonderry, Newry, Strabane, and Limavady, all heavily Catholic, have always been near the top of the unemployment tables. Each of them is on or near the geographical perimeter of Ulster and far from United Kingdom markets. Consequently, they are not attractive to industrial concerns and investors. How hard the government has tried to overcome this natural handicap, considering the religion of the local citizenry, is a hotly disputed issue. Nevertheless, the advent of large British and foreign firms to Ulster, wherever they are located, must eventually benefit the whole community. Such firms are unencumbered by historical religious preferences and refuse to discriminate.

PSYCHOLOGY

Fear is a predominant emotion in Ulster today. Nobody knows where the next bomb will go off or who will be its victims. People's nerves are constantly "on edge." Some psychiatrists say that many of the province's children and old people will never fully recover from the emotional trauma of the past few years. Yet fear is only one of two related emotions. The other is insecurity, and it lies at the very heart of the Irish problem. People in both communities feel that the principles they believe in and stand for are being called into question by events beyond their control. As a result they have reacted desperately, using extreme measures, in an attempt to protect the things they hold dear.

Let us consider the Protestants' feelings. They have three main concerns. First, they have little confidence that the rest of Britain understands their problems or is particularly committed to the cause of retaining Ulster within the United Kingdom. Most Protestants fervently believe that they are involved in a struggle against the forces of tyranny, anarchy, and Communism. And they are convinced that if such forces succeed in Ulster they will soon move against the rest of the United Kingdom. Yet they also know that many in Britain do not see things their way. To loyalists, the disbanding of the B-specials (in whom most had unquestioning faith and whose demise was felt to be a blatant example of political skulduggery), the desultory prosecution of the IRA by the army, the moves to try to have British troops recalled by an increasing number of English people, and the détente between British and Irish political leaders are all indicators that Britain's resolve to see the conflict through to a satisfactory conclusion is weak. Having endured many hardships to defend their British heritage, the loyalists feel betrayed because they realize that their fellow citizens will not support them unreservedly. The upsurge of Protestant support for a more hard-line position is evidence of the growing distrust with which English politicians are viewed. Recently, much of the Protestant antipathy toward the Liberal party (due to its previous attempts to introduce home rule) has been transferred to the British Labour party because of its statements about Ulster, its leaders, and its place in a united Ireland. At the same time Conservative party politicians have also fallen from favor.

Historically, the Conservative party has supported union with Britain, as indeed it still does. So when the government at Westminster closed down Stormont in 1972, assumed direct control of Ulster's affairs, insisted on political power-sharing in the new assembly, and dared to intern loyalists, the province was stunned—all the more so because the decisions were made by Conservatives. These decisions have so undermined the confidence of many loyalists that they no longer feel able to trust any English politicians or those who work within their guidelines. The recurrent talk of an Ulster unilateral declaration of independence is one result of this distrust; the demand for the return of Stormont is another. Only by following men who have proved their dependability, when so many others have proved untrustworthy, will Ulster Protestants feel secure.

Protestants generally do not so much want total independence as they dread the possible alternatives. At the moment, they feel unable democratically to influence their destiny. Their demand that there be no power-sharing in any new assembly, or, alternatively, that there be an executive with a large Protestant majority, really expresses their fear that unless they control the apparatus of power they may be sold out. Their opposition to a Council of Ireland stems from the same fear. Until a system is devised that provides the reassurance that a majority of them need, they will not seriously consider the province's future. And in the final analysis this need for reassurance may prove to be paramount. The irony of the present situation is that Protestants will not understand that their intransigence serves only to alienate the British and thus works against the very things they so desperately want.

The second insecurity is economic. The Protestants' dominance in Ulster rests in part on the fact that they have always controlled the economy. Traditionally, that economy was based on linen, ship-building, and agriculture. However, all of these industries are now declining, due to world-wide competition. Linen has been supplanted by man-made fibres; ship-building has decreased, but other countries have modernized their yards more quickly and now attract an increasing share of the business; small acreage farming simply does not pay in the modern world.

The consequences of these changes in Ulster have been high unemployment and continuous massive infusions of capital from Westminster. Neither of these factors has boosted Protestant self-confidence. The former is not only socially undesirable; it also increases economic pressure by raising the social security budget. At the same time, the unemployed—a high proportion of whom are Catholics —have the necessary time and motivation to foment trouble. Secondly, Ulster's financial dependence on Britain is now so great that the province has effectively lost economic control, and therefore political control, of its own future. This realization increases the Protestants' feelings of political insecurity, an insecurity supplemented by the difficulty in enticing replacement industries to a violent and divided land.

Finally, Protestants consider anyone who advocates or works for a united Ireland a direct and personal threat. This goal remains offensive and totally unacceptable to them for the political, theological, and social reasons already explained. And it may be that the strength of their feelings is increased by the suspicion that their refusal to compromise and join forces with the South is a losing cause. History seems to indicate that many movements similar to that for a united Ireland have eventually succeeded. Whatever the reasons, the Protestants' militant anti-Catholicism is bolstered by fear that the tide of social history will engulf Northern Ireland too. The insecurity that this uncertainty breeds, the belief that they are alone and caught up in a conflict they may not be able to win, could yet drive the Protestants to the ultimate extreme of total civil war in a last desperate attempt to secure the peace with justice they so passionately want.

Northern Ireland's Catholics are unhappy because they see themselves as second-class citizens in an alien and hostile society, and they point out that their physical safety was seriously threatened in 1969. While they may regret the loss of life resulting from IRA activities, many defend it as the only agency able and willing to protect them. In their view, even the army, whom they initially welcomed as liberators, turned out to be nothing more than repressive government agents. The insecurity of their status as Ulster citizens is frequently brought home to them. Within the framework of the law they are treated equally; yet they maintain that this equality does not obtain in practice. *The Cameron Commission's Report on Disturbances in Northern Ireland* stressed the role of local government grievances in formenting trouble. It commented on:

(1) A rising sense of continuing injustice and grievance among large sections of the Catholic population in Northern Ireland, in particular in Londonderry and Dungannon, in respect of (i) inadequacy of housing provision by certain local authorities, (ii) unfair methods of allocation of houses built and let by such authorities, in particular, refusals and omissions to adopt a "points" system in determining priorities and making allocations, (iii) misuse in certain cases of discretionary powers of allocation of houses in order to perpetuate Unionist control of the local authority. . . .

(2) Complaints, now well documented in fact, of discrimination in the making of local government appointments, at all levels but especially in senior posts, to the prejudice of non-Unionists and especially Catholic members of the community, in some Unionist controlled authorities. . . .

(3) Complaints, again well documented, in some cases of deliberate manipulation of local government electoral boundaries and in others a refusal to apply for their necessary extension, in order to achieve and maintain Unionist control of local authorities and so to deny to Catholics influence in local government proportionate to their numbers. . . .

(4) A growing and powerful sense of resentment and frustration among the Catholic population at failure to achieve either acceptance on the part of the Government of any need to investigate these complaints or to provide and enforce a remedy for them. . . .

In order that the above quotation not be misleading, one must be careful to note that the grievances in (1) were "in respect of certain local authorities" and the complaints in (2) and (3) were against "some" local authorities. Such authorities, it was made clear, were a minority. However, it is a sad fact that the actions of this minority have produced widespread resentment far beyond their local boundaries. Nor is this surprising if one believes that oppression by legally constituted authority is one of the most insidious forms of human debasement. Although these criticisms were accepted by Stormont and action was taken to correct them, the bitterness and frustration they caused cannot be banished with the stroke of a pen. Nor is it reasonable that Protestants should be indignant over the continuing resentment, bearing in mind how long the abuses were allowed to remain unchecked.

The initial use of the Special Powers Act almost exclusively against Catholics heightened the insecurity they already felt. To them internment was the ultimate weapon of a tyrannical government determined to suppress their legitimate, but in some cases violently illegal, opposition to that government. And the more recent jailing of Protestants has in no way assuaged their anger. Thus, the time came when even moderate Catholics found themselves driven to extremes—into the arms of the IRA—because they had no one else to trust. It could well be argued that the SDLP's contribution to peace has been its ability to reassure Catholics that their rights and their future can be protected legally and democratically.

It is axiomatic among many Catholics that economic history is repeating itself in Ulster. Just as England kept Ireland in economic subjection for centuries, they believe, Protestants are trying to keep them poor also. Many of them resent having to depend on the state and its social services for survival. They resent it first because the social security payments are vitally necessary to many of them. Yet Catholics are constantly aware that the payments are drawn from a community purse that is Protestant controlled. They may be subconsciously afraid that in a direct confrontation these necessary funds would be withheld. Secondly, they resent being dependent on subsidies from a state whose very existence a large number of them would like to destroy.

Those desiring work would claim that in seeking jobs they encounter employers with the mentality represented by Lord Brookeborough's remarks (cited earlier) or the mentality of the person who placed the following advertisement in a Belfast newspaper a few years ago: "Wanted—Reliable cook—general. Protestant (Christian preferred)." Catholics do "look after their own" also; they simply have less scope in which to do so and therefore come out of the battle of segregated economics less successfully. There can be little doubt that there are too few jobs with prospects of advancement to significant seniority and real fulfillment for Catholics. This constitutes a major factor in undermining their commitment to the province.

Finally, Catholic insecurity stems in part from their desire, latent or overt, to be part of a united Ireland. The clamor for instant reunification has diminished lately on both sides of the border, for political and economic reasons. The latter are particularly difficult to overcome with respect to the standards of living and social services available in the North and South. Northern Catholics would be much worse off economically if Ireland were to be reunited tomorrow. Nevertheless, the long-term desire of the people's hearts appears to be unshaken. And this eats away at the roots which a number of them have genuinely tried to put down in Ulster. For it is humanly impossible for a person to commit himself emotionally to one goal while at the same time he is striving to achieve an opposite one. Such competing loyalties invariably breed insecurity.

From Ulster's inception, when Catholics refused to cooperate in the founding of the state, they have generally held back part of themselves for Ireland. On the whole, they have not strived to be assimilated into the province, preferring rather to retain a separate and corporate identity. From their point of view, this desire to live lives centered in the church rather than the state and to aspire to a united Ireland is perfectly understandable and legitimate. However, it is equally understandable that it has evoked deep suspicion and resentful anger in those to whom the state means so much. Because of these attitudes, Ireland's future cannot be isolated from her past, regardless of how much any of us wishes it could.

The essayist Robert Lynd once wrote that all history is but a repetition of the same story with variations. In one important respect this was true of Catholics after the riots of August 12-14, 1969. In 1914, Irish politicians agreed to defer home rule, but some of their rank and file members refused to follow their lead and staged the 1916 rebellion. In 1921, the politicians accepted a political solution to the Irish problem, but a large sector of their constituents would not accept it and resorted to violence. In 1969, the official IRA in the North was advocating political change and eschewing violence. Yet the very violence of August 1969 undermined its authority; out of the ashes of Bombay Street arose the provisional IRA, who like their predecessors in 1916 and 1921 rejected words for the persuasion of the gun. Never again, they vowed, would Catholics try to accommodate with the hated Protestants; now they would take what they wanted by force. What has happened since that night is too painfully fresh in the memory to bear repeating in detail.

- The B-specials were disbanded and the police disarmed over Protestant protests.
- IRA gunmen took to the streets in a chilling battle with the army.

- The Ulster Defence Association became increasingly militant.
- More and more British troops went to Ulster—and were killed.
- Parts of Belfast and Derry became "no-go" areas and were subsequently "liberated" in Operation Motorman.
- Ordinary, harmless people died.
- There were allegations of and inquiries into army and police brutality.
- There was "Bloody Sunday," when citizens of Derry lost their lives after the army took offensive action to disperse crowds and seek out gunmen.
- There was "Bloody Friday," when Belfast suffered a reign of indiscriminate bombings.
- People hoped and then were disappointed when ceasefires lasted only a few weeks.
- There was and is internment.
- The government at Stormont was suspended, and a British minister of state was appointed to oversee the province.
- More people died.
- There were the Catholic rent strikes, tartan gangs, Vanguard, the Loyalist Association of Workers, the Catholic Women's Peace Committee, Sean MacStiophan's hunger strike, the Darlington Conference, the border plebiscite, the Abercorn restaurant bomb, backlash, Ulster freedom fighters, Communist arms, a new government in Dublin, the Price sisters, tar and feathers.
- The new Northern Ireland Assembly saw the election of three main political groupings, Unionists, Conservative Unionists (Paisleyites), who were against some of the British proposals that established them, and the Social Democratic and Labour party, the near unanimous voice of the Catholics. The moderate Alliance party substantially failed to draw voters away from their sectarian past, and the IRA was nowhere. The assembly failed and direct rule was reintroduced.

- The IRA bombing campaign moved to England.
- There were resentment, bitterness, and violence, endless discussion and argument, and millions of pounds' worth of damage.
- But overshadowing all else, hundreds of people were killed, maimed, and injured.

Life in Northern Ireland continues to be complex and unyielding. Two groups of people, with loyalties that affect their very beings, find themselves at loggerheads. They neither understand nor trust each other and make

Tar and feathers, one of the more severe disciplinary procedures extremists use to keep their members in line.

little attempt to do so, for each in his own way feels vulnerable. Perhaps it is unreasonable to expect that an eight-hundred-year-old problem will be solved in the space of a few months. Yet the suspicion lingers that unless Protestants and Catholics, Irishmen and Englishmen, stop blaming each other and start examining and reassessing the relative importance of the principles they hold dear, Ireland's future must remain shrouded in gloom and uncertainty.

An army Saladin scout car drives past Free Derry Corner, the rallying point of much past defiance of authority. This was a part of the moves in Belfast and Londonderry to clear barricades and regain control of "NO GO" areas, areas from which local inhabitants had excluded both the army and police for some time.

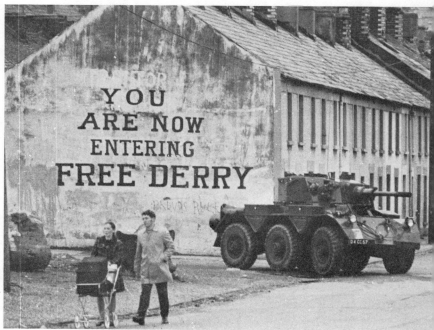

This boy, pictured during the Londonderry riots in 1969, is about to throw his "milk bottle petrol bomb" at the "enemy troops" in "his" country. The gas mask is to protect him from the army's tear gas response.

4 THE RELEVANCE OF CHRISTIANITY

THE REAL POLITICAL questions facing Ireland today are similar to the ones raised in America more than a century ago: What rights should a substantial and permanent minority possess in their dealings with the majority? Is democracy as we know it in Western civilization sensitive and flexible enough to protect minority interests? How can two communities, whose views are largely mutually exclusive, and yet who are forced to live together, reach a political accommodation acceptable to both? We believe that the only way in which such disparate groups can live together peacefully is through a willingness to accommodate and to compromise with each other. That necessity was finally recognized by Irish migrants and native Yankees in nineteenth-century America. It has still to be learned by their kinfolk at home during the latter part of the twentieth century.

The conflict in Northern Ireland is a microcosm of the difficulties of life in the modern Western world: the tensions that occur when the historic force of migration brings together people of different religions and races; the distortions in men's relationships when they respond to the competition for material goods in a society that places a high value on their attainment; the problems of operating a democracy when minorities seek to change the society by violent means. How Christianity fares in that context should be of interest to both Christians and non-Christians in Northern Ireland and throughout the world, because for all parties the question is the same: Does Christianity have any relevance?

We believe that Christianity *does* have a profound relevance for Northern Ireland, as it does for all mankind. Our aim in this final chapter is twofold: to suggest that a society of greater justice will obtain in Northern Ireland insofar as Christianity, as opposed to religion, becomes a predominant influence in the province; and to suggest that Christians should function "in the world" in order to witness to God's justice, the sort of justice he requires in his created world.

I

In an effort to understand Christianity's relevance to the future of Northern Ireland we must begin by considering the political options proposed for the province. Some of the options command more support than others, but listing all of them reveals the wide variety of opinions that currently exist.

    (a) a unilateral declaration of independence by Ulster, leaving no political ties with either Britain or Eire

    (b) a return to the pre-1968 status quo, i.e., effective government solely in Protestant hands

    (c) a total integration of Ulster with the rest of the United Kingdom, in the manner of Wales and Scotland

    (d) the establishment of an executive within a new Northern Ireland Assembly in which Protestant and Catholic participation would be proportionate to their respective political strengths

    (e) a federated all-Ireland republic in which regional

parliaments in Belfast and Dublin would retain substantial control over regional matters, while both would yield other powers to a federal parliament in regard to "national" matters

(f) a socialist all-Ireland republic in which the traditional politics of both Belfast and Dublin would be entirely swept away

(g) a total integration of Ulster with the rest of Ireland under a liberal, secular constitution

Throughout this book we have tried to portray objectively the views of the two sides in the conflict as fairly as possible. We have no intention of departing from that practice at this stage. Nevertheless, a few comments on each of these options from a Christian perspective is appropriate.

There are two peoples living in Ireland, each of whom has historic identities, rights, and interests that must be safeguarded constitutionally. If they are not so protected, the integrity of the individuals in one or both groups will inevitably be undermined. We believe that such a damaging process is a denial of the whole basis of Christianity. As a result, Christians should feel unable to support any political arrangements that do not uphold all aspects of human dignity.

In view of the annual grant from the British exchequer of around 400 million pounds (one billion dollars), it is highly doubtful that Ulster could sustain independence —proposal (a)—especially since it has always been assumed that such an independence would be Protestant dominated as would be the arrangements envisioned in proposal (b). Proposal (f) is supported by only a small minority of extreme republicans. Christian concern, should any of these proposals be adopted, would center on the social and constitutional arrangements likely to prevail under them. The new constitutions would probably not recognize the need to give full civil rights to all people. In fact, for the new state to survive under these proposals, its constitution would almost certainly have to suppress a sizable permanent minority and deprive them of effective means of legally influencing their destiny. Christians, however, must oppose the notion that numerical superiority and might make right.

Any of the other four proposals might, in principle, be acceptable to Christians, depending on the details that ultimately emerged. Proposal (c) has the advantage that it would more effectively guarantee the "Britishness" of Ulster on the one hand, and the civil rights of its minority on the other. Its drawback is that many persons in the rest of Great Britain would see it as blocking their desire to be rid of Ireland once and for all. Proposal (d), which was essentially the assembly system plus representation of the more loyalist elements, and (e) both recognize the essential differences existing among Irish people. In different ways they seek to bring the two groups together while allowing both to retain their historic identities, rights, and interests. Finally, proposal (g) would require a much greater degree of separation between church and state in the Irish Republic than presently obtains. If this were successfully accomplished and accompanied by economic measures to ensure that Ulster people suffered no decrease in the standards of their social services, then in principle there would be no Christian basis for opposing this proposal. Its adoption, however, is not now a viable alternative, irrespective of whether or not it should ever be so.

Having said this, we would like to reassert emphatically that we have no prescription for the political and social future of the Irish peoples. We say only that, given the historic presence of two peoples on the island, the only way in which they may begin to live together in peace is to acknowledge that they are different peoples, and to recognize and guarantee constitutionally that the aspirations of both communities, if they cannot be mutually realized, can and must be accorded equal and legitimate redress of grievances. If Ireland is to have a future, some consensus must emerge in which majorities of the two peoples decide that they can live and work together.

II

As Christians we believe that all men are created in the image of God, and although the fact of sin has tarnished that image, it has not been erased. This belief is so basic to Christianity that all Christians, regardless of sectarian differences, must surely share it. Thus, if men bear the image of God, they all have equal worth in his sight. God is not a respecter of persons: from his viewpoint we are a community of equals. The Decalogue given in the Old Testament was intended to guide us in our communal living and to provide for us a framework within which we are all accountable to God. The New Testament extension of the law by Jesus Christ expresses accountability not only to God but to each other. The commands to do unto others as one would have them do to him, and to love one's neighbor as himself, are a reflection of the grace of God incarnated in Christ and known through faith in him. Throughout the Bible, moreover, there is no suggestion that God expects some people to be accorded greater or lesser respect or dignity.

On the other hand, while men are equal they are not the same, and we should value individual differences as assiduously as God does. Therefore, when men come to organize their societies, they must preserve man's created equality as well as his individual differences. Such a society of justice will not admit to one faction's holding predominant sway over another, nor to one faction's requiring the others to reject the differences that stem from their humanity. We believe that God abhors tyranny, whether it be the tyranny of the bomb and bullet, of discriminatory legislation, of intimidation and coercion, or of the denial of freedom of worship. God requires justice, and justice cannot coexist with tyranny. The forms that God's justice will take certainly vary with time and place, and they must be determined and reappraised regularly. Whatever the societal forms under which Christians live, however, we believe that because of their faith commitment they must seek to promote as much justice as possible under those forms; that justice, however formulated, will promote the equality of men while safeguarding their individuality, both of which are precious in God's sight. With specific reference to Northern Ireland, constitutional forms that would promote justice should enjoy Christian favor. Similarly, any and all forms that would limit or prevent justice should be unacceptable to Christians.

We realize that the presence of sin retards the accomplishment of justice on this earth. Consequently, social justice will be more nearly approximated as men are changed through being reconciled to God by Christ. Yet this suggestion broaches the most difficult aspect of the conflict in Northern Ireland. As previously noted, Ulster has a higher percentage of church-going people than most other parts of the world. In light of this, we are faced with two genuinely perplexing problems. Why has all of Northern Ireland's religion not caused an improvement in social relations over the years? Why has it instead become the axis of the conflict? Critics might well scoff, pointing out that we are suggesting that "religion has failed—give us more religion." The only honest response to such criticism is to admit that the critic is correct in alleging that religion has failed. What we are calling for, however, is not more religion. We are rather calling for Christianity, acknowledging that religion is not the same as Christianity.

The authors of this book have had similar experiences both in Britain and the United States in talking with people about the role of religion and Christianity in "the troubles." Many critics of Christianity believe that we would do better to be "worldly," to live together in peace, rather than be the kind of "Christians" who cannot live with each other. We have heard several people suggest that Ulster would be much better off if Christianity were abolished. Television documentaries, shown in both Britain and America, speak of "Christians at war," and it may appear to many people throughout the world that this phrase sums up what is happening in Northern Ireland today. We could submit that such a viewpoint is mistaken, again because religion is not the same as Christianity.

Defining a Christian is not difficult. A Christian is one who acknowledges before God his sinfulness and his inability to rectify his condition. He believes that Jesus Christ's claim to the Son of God is true, and that Christ is the only way by which he can be brought back to God. He believes in Christ's substitutionary death and resurrection. As a result of the Christian's act of faith, the Spirit of God dwells in him and becomes the motivating force in his life—a life dedicated to serving God in whatever area of life is his "calling," and in all his human relationships.

Defining a "religious" person, however, is more difficult. For reasons not altogether clear, there is a large number of people who either agree to church membership or give nominal assent to the "belief system" of Christianity without considering the claims of God on their lives. It is not our purpose to judge these people, whether in Ireland, Britain, or America; we only observe that they exist—a fact Jesus anticipated when he noted that there would be on the final day many pseudo-believers who would protest vigorously their religious loyalty.

The fact is that substantial confusion exists in the minds of many persons, both in Europe and America, both inside and outside the church, on this matter of distinguishing between "Christian" and "religious." Also, the universal

usage of the terms "Protestant" and "Catholic" in Northern Ireland, without regard for theological accuracy,
tends to mask the reality that in both groups there are
Christians as well as religious people. In both Protestant
and Catholic religious groups one can identify (a) religious church-goers, (b) Christians, and (c) those who seldom if ever attend church. The last, while essentially
irreligious, will happily accept a denominational label
because they believe it describes their heritage. The first
are the large number of "religious" people who would
call themselves "Christian" (and would call Ulster a
"Christian" nation), but whose definition of Christianity
does not intersect with the biblical one.

We would like to emphasize that we believe these divisions occur within *both* Protestant and Catholic groups;
and because this is so, it is invalid to portray the religious/
Christian dimension of Ulster's problems in simple sectarian terms. Even less acceptable is the suggestion that
Christianity is at the root of the conflict; indeed, we would
suggest that precisely the opposite is so. Unfortunately,
however, these distinctions are not always clear in the
public mind, and if Christians do not make them clear,
Christianity will continue to be brought into disrepute by
the "religious" connections of Northern Ireland.

III

No Christian finds it easy to say publicly what makes him
different from "religious" people. His nominally believing,
church-attending friends may be upset by the claim of a
personal faith in Jesus Christ they do not share. They may
think him arrogant and divisive, and may even withhold
valued friendship, thus contributing to social tension. In
the face of circumstances such as these, the temptation to
say nothing and simply to try "to live a good witness"

becomes very strong. When faced with this temptation, it is important to remember that Jesus commanded his disciples to go and *tell* all nations the good news of the gospel. By explaining and interpreting the life and death of Jesus the disciples could transmit clearly the message of salvation to those who had not known him. (Of course, words had to be verified with consistent behavior to have credibility.) Jesus also wished to establish visibly and identifiably the kingdom of God on earth. That is to say, by witnessing to the gospel the disciples forthrightly declared their allegiance to Christ and his righteousness, thereby setting themselves apart from the rest of the "world." Unless believers today identify themselves with God in a similarly unmistakable way, the whole basis of Christian protest both within and outside the religious community is undermined. Those who are continually unwilling to stand up for their faith make ineffective spokesmen for Jesus Christ when it becomes necessary to divorce Christianity from those acts performed in the name of "religion."

If it is difficult for us to become identifiable Christians within our own religious communities, the problems are immense in formulating an acceptable witness to those in different denominational communities. People in sympathy with our spiritual motivation may still not understand our concern to cross sectarian lines and may even deliberately misinterpret it. Rigid religio-sociological divisions can make it very difficult to have fellowship with other Christians, because pressure is always present to conform to the traditions of our forefathers. Any move toward the "other side" in a tense situation such as that in Northern Ireland, even on an individual basis, often renders a Christian doctrinally and politically suspect in the eyes of both his friends and his enemies.

These reasons for restricting the scope of Christian witness, while fully understandable from the human point of view, must be seen in contrast to our theological base. By the inflexible separation of the Christians of Northern Ireland into Protestant and Catholic groups the body of Christ has been divided—and this world-wide division tears relentlessly at the oneness and unity that all believers should enjoy in Jesus Christ. We recognize, of course, that the theological and doctrinal differences are real and profound and cannot be wished away by desires for Christian unity. Indeed, it is precisely the depth and breadth of those differences, when allied to political principles and practices, that have created a situation in which many Christians have become isolated within their own sectarian communities. However, being mindful of the difficulties, we suggest that Christians must nevertheless try to overcome them. While not ignoring the real differences that exist, Christians must realize that they do have a unifying factor: those who love and trust in Jesus Christ share "one Lord, one faith, one birth." The onus is on all Christians to seek areas of reconciliation in which this pre-eminent fact of their lives can be given expression. Christian believers are the best hope for Northern Ireland because only they, both Protestant and Catholic, have a bond that genuinely transcends sectarian strife.

It should not be assumed from the above that Protestants and Catholics in Ulster never interact with each other. There are many good neighbors and friends who pay scant attention to each other's denominational affiliation. Some Protestant and Catholic clergymen and laity have begun informally meeting and praying together, and the charismatic movement is observable in both communities. All of these interactions tend to reduce the barriers between the communities, and they offer the brightest rays of hope for Northern Ireland. This hope is not necessarily for ecclesiastical union, and certainly not for the return of the "erring" Protestant sheep to the fold of Rome; but it lies in the fellowship of groups of individual Christians and in the outpouring of the Spirit of God in the hearts of those who love, trust, and seek to obey God.

There is a consensus among those who comment on religion in Northern Ireland that doctrinal purity has been critically important to both sides' attempts to render "truth," with the result that the doctrinal gulf between them is not only wide but sharply defined. Even "religious" people defend their side's view with a passion that is difficult to understand, since they have little or no spiritual commitment to it. Consequently, one characteristic of Jesus Christ, which would normally be expected to differentiate between "religious" men and Christians, has been ignored. John wrote of Christ that he was "full of grace and truth." The context in which this observation occurs suggests that these were the two definitive aspects of his character. Those of us in the world community of Christians who would seek an imitation of Christ stand condemned insofar as our quest for doctrinal truth has not been balanced with this desire for grace. We do not have a winsomeness of spirit toward those who disagree with us. We show little loving tolerance toward those who interpret Scripture differently than we do. The meekness, kindness, and generosity exemplifying Jesus' attitude toward his "enemies" is sadly an attitude that is imitated very poorly by his followers. In a situation where doctrinal issues are hotly debated—as in Northern Ireland— the graceless tendency we all recognize within ourselves is frequently taken to its extreme.

What John meant by grace is what Paul meant by "the fruit of the spirit"—the evidence of a God-centered and God-controlled life. It is this which has to be added to the Christian's claim to have a distinctive message if the world is to recognize that Jesus Christ is Lord. Only then will people realize that any Christianity that is Christ-less is little more than a sociological category, and that its adherents are basically no different from the rest of humanity.

IV

We acknowledge, however, that many "religious" people in Northern Ireland may not turn to the "newness of life in Christ," even though we pray that they will. But saying this is not to concede that Christianity will consequently have no relevance in Ulster. On the contrary, we would re-emphasize that all Christians, by the very nature of their faith commitment, are thrust into the social and political arena and must work for justice within it. It is not a matter of *either* preaching the individual gospel of salvation *or* working for social justice. It seems clear to us that the Christian is called to do both.

In the Sermon on the Mount, Jesus described Christians as "the salt of the earth"—a description opposing any suggestions that they may opt out of society. Nor was Jesus' requirement of Christian social involvement an option the believer was free to choose or reject. Christianity entails not only an individual's personal relationship with God but also involves the totality of his life on this earth. In this sense we see no distinctions between the callings of "full-time Christian service." There are no distinctions because no human activities are more or less important in the total witness that Christians should bring to the world. This is so because the redemption of the world depends ultimately on the sovereign purposes of God; and these purposes are now advanced by and through the total witness of his people. As his people, therefore, Christians must witness to God's grace and to his kingdom, which will surely come.

The important point for our present discussion is that God's kingdom is not merely a spiritual one confined to men's hearts. The Christian message points to a kingdom that lays claim to every aspect of human life, and that includes political structures. As Richard J. Mouw has written in *Political Evangelism:*

The New Testament's use of a political metaphor to describe the sum of God's redemptive purposes indicates that the total transformation of all things which God intends for his creation includes a transformation of the political realm. . . . The political sphere is not merely an area in which a Christian *can* be a witness; it is one in which we are *called* to proclaim the liberating power of the gospel.

A word of caution is in order here. It is easy for any person to sit in judgment on other people. Most of us can see the flaws in others while overlooking our own glaring faults. Yet Jesus commanded that we not judge others lest we ourselves be judged. Thus, it is not our purpose to criticize or censure the Christians of Northern Ireland. Any conclusions that we may draw concerning their attitudes and behavior are based on the premise that, if Christianity has relevance for Northern Ireland, it must apply to the observers as well as to the observed. When we engage in the quest for Christian social justice, we must be careful not to preface our own ideas with "thus saith the Lord." As Christians, we must recognize our own fallibility, and we should not dogmatically identify specific proposals for Northern Ireland's future as the will of God. Both the goal and our method of seeking it should reflect the character and teaching of God and should accord with his revealed purposes. The only political and social systems Christians can support will, by their nature, allow people to be treated equally and fairly and will recognize their individual and collective differences. In the final analysis it must be the peoples of Northern Ireland who come together in some workable consensus on which a majority of them agree.

Finally, we say: Let there be peace in Northern Ireland. Even as we acknowledge that peace is more likely to come as individuals begin working together as Christians, rather than as Protestants and Catholics, we also plead that all Christians—in Ulster, Eire, Britain, the United States, and Canada—begin praying for and witnessing not only to individuals but to institutional structures about the liberating power of the gospel. If such collective witnessing could begin, we would all be closer to the day in which we will no longer have to bear the burden of Northern Ireland. In pointing to the coming kingdom of God, we will be pointing to a political and social situation in which the kingdoms of the world will become the kingdoms of our Lord and of his Christ, and in which every knee shall bow in declaration of Christ's lordship, and in which there is no Greek or Jew, no Protestant or Catholic, no bond or free, but his people will be a fellowship that will "glorify God and enjoy him forever."

SUGGESTIONS FOR FURTHER READING

Barritt, D.P. and Carter, C.F., *The Northern Ireland Problem.* London: Oxford University Press, 1962.

Beckett, J.C., *A Short History of Ireland.* London: Hutchinson University Library, 1973 (5th ed.).

Boyd, A., *Holy War in Belfast.* Dublin: Anvil Books, 1969.

Duffy, J., *The Irish in the United States.* Belmont, Calif.: Wadsworth, 1971.

Handlin, O., *Boston's Immigrants.* Cambridge, Mass.: Harvard University Press, 1959 (rev. ed.).

Kennedy, E.M., "Ulster is an International Issue," *Foreign Policy,* Number 11 (Summer, 1973), 57-71.

Mouw, R., *Political Evangelism.* Grand Rapids: Eerdmans, 1974.

Report of the Cameron Commission on Disturbance in Northern Ireland. Her Majesty's Stationery Office, 1969.

Wallace, M., *Northern Ireland — Fifty Years of Self-government.* Newton Abbot: David and Charles, 1971; New York: Barnes & Noble, 1971.

Wittke, C., *The Irish in America.* Baton Rouge: Louisiana State University Press, 1956.